Company's Coming ®

HOLIDAY ENTERTAINING

by
Jean Paré

HOLIDAY ENTERTAINING

Eighth Edition February 1990

I.S.B.N. 0-9690695-7-X

Published and Distributed by
Company's Coming Publishing Limited
Box 8037, Station ''F''
Edmonton, Alberta, Canada
T6H 4N9

Printed in Canada

Cookbooks in the Company's Coming series by Jean Paré:

150 DELICIOUS SQUARES

CASSEROLES

MUFFINS & MORE

SALADS

APPETIZERS

DESSERTS

SOUPS & SANDWICHES

HOLIDAY ENTERTAINING

COOKIES

JEAN PARÉ'S FAVORITES VOLUME ONE

VEGETABLES

MAIN COURSES

PASTA

CAKES (SEPTEMBER, 1990)

table of Contents

the Jean Paré story

Jean Paré was born and raised during the Great Depression in Irma, a small farm town in eastern Alberta. She grew up understanding that the combination of family, friends and home cooking is the essence of a good life. Jean learned from her mother, Ruby Elford, to appreciate good cooking and was encouraged by her father, Edward Elford, who praised even her earliest attempts. When she left home she took with her many acquired family recipes, her love of cooking and her intriguing desire to read recipe books like novels!

While raising a family of four, Jean was always busy in her kitchen preparing delicious, tasty treats and savory meals for family and friends of all ages. Her reputation flourished as the mom who could happily feed the neighborhood.

In 1963, when her children had all reached school age, Jean volunteered to cater to the 50th anniversary of the Vermilion School of Agriculture, now Lakeland College. Working out of her home, Jean prepared a dinner for over 1000 people which launched a flourishing catering operation that continued for over eighteen years. During that time she was provided with countless opportunities to test new ideas with immediate feedback – resulting in empty plates and contented customers! Whether preparing cocktail sandwiches for a house party or serving a hot meal for 1500 people, Jean Paré earned a reputation for good food, courteous service and reasonable prices.

"Why don't you write a cookbook?" Time and again Jean was asked that question as requests for her recipes mounted. Jean's response was to team up with her son Grant Lovig in the fall of 1980 to form Company's Coming Publishing Limited. April 14, 1981 marked the debut of "150 DELICIOUS SQUARES", the first Company's Coming cookbook in what soon would become Canada's most popular cookbook series. Jean released a new title each year for the first six years. The pace quickened and by 1987 the company had begun publishing two titles each year.

Jean Paré's operation has grown from the early days of working out of a spare bedroom in her home to operating a large and fully equipped test kitchen in Vermilion, near the home she and her husband Larry built. Full time staff has grown steadily to include marketing personnel located in major cities across Canada. Home office is located in Edmonton, Alberta where distribution, accounting and administration functions are headquartered. Company's Coming cookbooks are now distributed throughout Canada and the United States plus numerous overseas markets.

Jean Paré's approach to cooking has always called for easy-to-follow recipes using mostly common, affordable ingredients. Her wonderful collection of time-honored recipes, many of which are family heirlooms, are a welcome addition to any kitchen. That's why we say: taste the tradition.

Holiday entertaining. My thoughts turn to family,
friends and festive occasions. Taste the tradition!

ℱoreword

The next best thing to a holiday is holiday food. What better time than a holiday to gather friends and family for a festive occasion?

This book features complete menus for holidays and special events throughout the year. From Thanksgiving and Christmas to Valentine's Day and Halloween, enjoy the convenience of taste-tested, preplan–ned menus. Complete or partial menus may be easily interchanged. A variety of complimentary recipes round off the selection. The index is cross-referenced to assist you when planning meals.

Preceeding each menu is a preamble made up of suggestions for decorations, choice of colors plus loads of reasons for holiday enter–taining.

Holidays bring out the best of our traditions. We tend to associate certain dishes with particular holidays, but we should also be open to trying something new. Holiday entertaining will provide you with ample opportunity to expand your horizons. So when company's coming, make it special. Taste the tradition!

Jean Paré

NEW YEAR'S DAY

The very first holiday of the new year also brings to a close the festive season of the previous year. It is fitting that such a joyous time should end with a new beginning.

If your plans include viewing televised sporting events, a buffet meal is in order. Otherwise, an elegant sit-down meal is a terrific way to wind up the holiday season.

For a buffet meal, begin with several of the listed hors d'oeuvres, followed later with Baron Of Beef, Cajun Style, sliced for buns, Pasta or Potato Salad, Cucumber Salad or any of the many suggestions found throughout this book.

Above all else, try not to break all of your New Year's resolutions on the first day!

MENU

Cream of Carrot Soup

Glazed Ham

Scalloped Potatoes
Sweet Potato Casserole
Celery Casserole
Harvard Beets

Creamy Coleslaw
Vegetable Mold

Chocolate Orange Cheesecake

CREAM OF CARROT SOUP

Smooth and soothing. A sure hit.

Butter or margarine	¼ cup	50 mL
Medium onions, chopped	2	2
Garlic clove, minced	1	1
Medium potatoes, diced	3	3
Medium carrots, diced	4	4
Chicken stock	5 cups	1.1 L
Bay leaf	1	1
Thyme	¼ - ½ tsp.	1 - 2 mL
Pepper	¼ tsp.	1 mL

Melt butter in large saucepan. Add onion and garlic. Sauté until clear and soft.

Add remaining ingredients using smaller amount of thyme. Bring to a boil. Cover and simmer until vegetables are tender. Discard bay leaf. Add more thyme if desired. Makes 8½ cups (2 L).

PINEAPPLE SAUCE

A perfect condiment to serve with ham.

Crushed pineapple with juice	14 oz.	398 mL
Granulated sugar	1 cup	250 mL
Water	1 cup	250 mL
Lemon juice	2 tbsp.	30 mL
Cornstarch	2 tbsp.	30 mL

Measure all ingredients into medium size saucepan. Heat and stir until it boils and thickens. Serve hot or cold. Makes approximately 3 cups (700 mL).

Pictured on page 17.

Variation: Use brown sugar instead of white. The end result is a darker color and a slight caramel flavor.

GLAZED HAM

Glazed to perfection for a traditional Easter.

Ham, bone in, rind on	**6 lbs.**	**2.7 kg**
Brown sugar	**½ cup**	**125 mL**
Mustard powder	**1 tsp.**	**5 mL**
Condensed frozen orange juice	**3 tbsp.**	**50 mL**
Whole cloves		
Pineapple chunks		
Maraschino cherries, halved		

With sharp knife, score rind in triangle pattern about ¼ inch (1 cm) deep. Place ham in roaster. Cover. Bake in 350°F (180°C) oven for 2 hours. Remove from oven and cut rind off ham. Increase oven heat to 450°F (230°C).

Push a whole clove into each triangle. Secure pineapple and cherry halves with toothpicks. Place here and there over ham. Mix sugar and mustard powder together. Add concentrated orange juice and mix to a paste. Brush over surface of ham.

Bake uncovered about 15 minutes to glaze. In about half time, spoon drippings over surface again. Serves 8.

Note: This recipe uses a ready to serve ham. Internal temperature should read 140°F (60°C) when done. Other hams should reach an internal temperature of 160°F (70°C).

Pictured on page 17.

When you are finally old enough to know all the answers, nobody asks you any questions.

SCALLOPED POTATOES

A quick and easy way to fix a super tasting dish.

Thinly sliced potatoes	8 cups	1.8 L
Thinly sliced onion	1 cup	250 mL
Condensed cream of mushroom soup	20 oz.	568 mL
Milk	1 cup	250 mL
Salt	½ tsp.	2 mL
Pepper	⅛ tsp.	0.5 mL
Paprika sprinkle		

Layer potato and onion in 3 quart (3.5 L) casserole.

Mix soup, milk, salt and pepper together. Pour over top. Insert spoon here and there to allow some sauce to penetrate.

Sprinkle with paprika. Bake covered in 375°F (190°C) oven for about 1 hour, 15 minutes or until tender. Remove cover during last 10 minutes. Serves 8.

SWEET POTATO CASSEROLE

May be prepared ahead. Just reheat and serve. This has a beautiful glaze.

Sweet potatoes, peeled, cooked and cut into irregular shaped pieces	2½ lbs.	1.1 kg
Brown sugar, packed	½ cup	125 mL
Butter or margarine	2 tbsp.	30 mL
Cornstarch	1½ tbsp.	25 mL
Salt	½ tsp.	2 mL
Pepper	⅛ tsp.	0.5 mL
Prepared orange juice	1 cup	250 mL

Cut potatoes into bite size pieces and place in 2 quart (2 L) casserole.

Mix remaining ingredients in saucepan. Heat and stir until it boils and thickens. Pour over potatoes. Cover and bake in 350°F (180°C) oven for 20 minutes. Remove cover for last few minutes if desired. Serves 8.

Pictured on page 17.

Note: This can be made using 2 cans, 19 oz. (540 mL) each, drained sweet potatoes, cut into chunks.

CELERY CASSEROLE

Combined with eggs, this is a creamy dish. Try your celery hot for a change.

Sliced celery, boiled tender	2 cups	500 mL
Hard-boiled eggs, sliced or chopped	2	2
Instant onion flakes	1 tbsp.	15 mL
Butter or margarine	2 tbsp.	30 mL
All-purpose flour	2 tbsp.	30 mL
Salt	1/2 tsp.	2 mL
Pepper	1/8 tsp.	0.5 mL
Milk	1 cup	250 mL
Butter or margarine	2 tbsp.	30 mL
Dry bread crumbs	1/2 cup	125 mL

Put drained celery into 8 inch (20 cm) casserole. Arrange egg slices over top. Sprinkle with onion flakes.

Melt butter in saucepan. Mix in flour, salt and pepper. Add milk stirring until it boils and thickens. Pour over celery mixture.

Melt butter in saucepan. Stir in crumbs. Sprinkle over sauce in cas-serole. Bake uncovered in 350°F (180°C) until browned and hot, about 20 to 30 minutes. Serves 6 to 8.

Variation: Sprinkle with cheese half way through baking.

HARVARD BEETS

A good way to get youngsters to eat beets.

Beets, drain, reserve juice	14 oz.	398 mL
Granulated sugar	1/4 cup	50 mL
Cornstarch	1 tbsp.	15 mL
Salt	1/4 tsp.	1 mL
Beet juice	1/2 cup	125 mL
Cider vinegar	1/4 cup	50 mL

Dice beets and set aside.

In small saucepan mix sugar, cornstarch, salt, beet juice and vinegar. Cook and stir over medium heat until it boils and thickens. Add beets and heat through. Serves 4. Double recipe to serve 8.

Note: To make sauce for fresh beets, use water instead of beet juice.

VEGETABLE MOLD

Full of vegetables. Good color. Good taste. This is suitable for making individual salad molds.

Lime flavored gelatin	3 oz.	85 g
Boiling water	1 cup	225 mL
Cold water	3/4 cup	175 mL
Shredded cabbage	1 cup	250 mL
Chopped celery	1/2 cup	125 mL
Shredded carrot	1/2 cup	125 mL
Sweet pickle relish	1/4 cup	50 mL
Chopped pimiento	2 tbsp.	30 mL

Dissolve gelatin in boiling water. Add cold water. Chill until syrupy.

Add remaining ingredients. Fold into gelatin evenly. Spoon into salad mold. Chill. Makes about 3 cups (700 mL). Serves 8.

Pictured on page 17.

CREAMY COLESLAW

A fine textured slaw that doesn't take forever to chew. Allow extra as more of this is usually eaten by everyone.

Finely grated cabbage	4 cups	900 mL
Finely grated carrot	1	1
Salad dressing such as Miracle Whip	1 1/4 cups	275 mL
Granulated sugar	3 1/4 tsp.	15 mL
Prepared mustard	2 tsp.	10 mL

Grate cabbage and carrot into large bowl. Set aside.

Mix salad dressing, sugar and mustard together. Add to cabbage–carrot mixture. Stir well to mix. Serves 8.

Note: Cabbage and carrot may be grated the day before. Cover and chill. Shortly before serving, mix them with dressing mixture.

CHOCOLATE ORANGE CHEESECAKE

No New Year's resolution can stand up to this.

CRUST

Butter or margarine	¼ cup	50 mL
Graham cracker crumbs	1 cup	250 mL
Granulated sugar	2 tbsp.	30 mL
Cocoa	3 tbsp.	50 mL

FILLING

Cream cheese, softened	2 x 8 oz.	2 x 250 g
Granulated sugar	1¼ cups	300 mL
Eggs	4	4
Frozen concentrated orange juice	¼ cup	60 mL
Semisweet chocolate chips	1½ cups	375 mL
Vanilla	1 tsp.	5 mL
Orange flavoring	1 tsp.	5 mL

Crust: Melt butter in saucepan. Stir in crumbs, sugar and cocoa. Mix well. Press into bottom of ungreased 9 inch (22 cm) springform pan. Bake in 350°F (180°C) oven for 10 minutes.

Filling: Beat cream cheese and sugar at low speed until blended. Add eggs, 1 at a time, beating slowly after each addition. Mix in concen-trated orange juice.

Melt chocolate chips in saucepan over low heat. Stir to hasten melt-ing. Add to cheese mixture. Add flavorings. Pour into crumb-lined pan. Bake in 325°F (160°C) oven for 70 minutes until top feels firm and dry. Cake will quiver if pan is shaken slightly. Cool at room tem-perature, then chill several hours or overnight before serving. Serves 8 to 10.

Pare Pointer

The hardest thing about learning how to skate is the ice.

Just the jellied salad to serve with ham. Tangy and smooth as satin.
Make the day before.

Eggs	4	4
Water	½ cup	125 mL
Cider vinegar	¾ cup	175 mL
Granulated sugar	¾ cup	175 mL
Unflavored gelatin powder	¼ oz.	7 g
Turmeric	1 tsp.	5 mL
Salt	¼ tsp.	1 mL
Dry mustard powder	3 tbsp.	50 mL
Whipping cream (or 1 env. topping)	1 cup	250 mL

Beat eggs together well in top of double boiler. Stir in water and vinegar. Set aside.

Measure sugar into medium size bowl. Add gelatin, turmeric, salt and mustard powder. Stir all together until thoroughly mixed. Add to egg mixture and mix. Place over boiling water. Cook and stir until thick‐ened slightly. Remove from heat and cool until mixture is syrupy thick.

Beat cream until stiff. Fold into thickened jelly. Then pour into 4 cup (900 mL) mold. Chill several hours.

Is it a coincidence that the word improvement begins "I"?

RAISIN SAUCE

Serve with baked ham, also with boiled or broiled ham.

Raisins	½ cup	125 mL
Hot water	2 cups	500 mL
Brown sugar, packed	1⅓ cups	325 mL
Cornstarch	¼ cup	60 mL
Water	½ cup	125 mL
Vinegar	3 tbsp.	50 mL
Dry mustard powder	¼ tsp.	1 mL

Put raisins and hot water in medium saucepan. Let stand 1 hour.

Stir in brown sugar and cornstarch. Add water, vinegar and mustard. Heat and stir over medium heat until boiled and thickened. Serve with ham. Makes 2 cups (500 mL).

NEW YEAR'S DAY

PEANUT SQUARES

This chocolaty goodie is a snap to make. Freezes well.

FIRST LAYER

Smooth peanut butter	1 cup	250 mL
Semisweet chocolate chips	1 cup	250 mL
Butterscotch chips	1 cup	250 mL

SECOND LAYER

Butter or margarine	½ cup	125 mL
Vanilla custard powder	2 tbsp.	30 mL
Evaporated milk	¼ cup	60 mL
Icing (confectioner's) sugar	3 cups	750 mL
Maple flavoring	½ tsp.	2 mL

THIRD LAYER
Reserved peanut butter mixture

Peanuts	1 cup	250 mL

First Layer: Combine peanut butter and all chips in saucepan. Heat over low heat stirring often until smooth. Spread ½ mixture over ungreased 9 × 13 inch (22 × 33 cm) pan. Chill until firm. Keep second ½ mixture for third layer.

Second Layer: Measure butter, custard powder and milk in saucepan. Heat and stir until it reaches a full rolling boil. Remove from heat. Add icing sugar and flavoring. Stir until mixture forms into ball. Cool to room temperature. Using spoon and your hand press in smooth layer over firm chocolate base.

Third Layer: To reserved mixture add peanuts. Stir and spread over second layer. Chill. Cut into 54 squares.

Pictured on page 143.

NOODLE STACKS

Irregular little heaps of temptation.

Semisweet chocolate chips	1 cup	250 mL
Butterscotch chips	1 cup	250 mL
Peanuts	1 cup	250 mL
Chinese noodles	2 cups	500 mL

Melt chocolate and butterscotch chips in fairly large saucepan over low heat.

Stir in peanuts and dry noodles. Drop on waxed paper to cool. Makes about 2 dozen.

FIVE MINUTE FUDGE

Fast and foolproof. Creamy.

Butter or margarine	2 tbsp.	30 mL
Evaporated milk	⅔ cup	150 mL
Granulated sugar	1⅔ cups	375 mL
Salt	½ tsp.	2 mL
Tiny marshmallows	2 cups	500 mL
Semisweet chocolate chips	1½ cups	350 mL
Vanilla	1 tsp.	5 mL
Chopped walnuts	½ cup	125 mL

Put butter, milk, sugar and salt in medium size saucepan over medium heat. Bring to boil. Boil 5 minutes stirring continually. Remove from heat.

Add remaining ingredients. Stir to mix. Then beat with spoon 1 minute. Marshmallows should be melted. Pour into greased 8 × 8 inch (20 × 20 cm) pan. Cool. Cut into 36 squares. Makes about 2 pounds (900 g).

Pictured on page 143.

DIVINITY FUDGE

Makes a white smooth confection. Divine.

Granulated sugar	3 cups	750 mL
Boiling water	1 cup	250 mL
Light corn syrup	½ cup	125 mL
Salt	⅛ tsp.	0.5 mL
Egg whites	2	2
Vanilla	1 tsp.	5 mL
Cherries, cut up	½ cup	125 mL

Put sugar, water, syrup and salt into heavy saucepan. Stir over medium heat until dissolved. Boil slowly, without stirring, until hard ball stage 260°F (128°C), or until a small amount dropped into ice water forms a hard ball that is still pliable.

(continued on next page)

Just before hard ball stage is reached, beat egg whites in good size bowl until stiff. Pour syrup mixture slowly in a thin stream into egg whites beating all the time until almost stiff. When it appears dull and a small spoonful will hold its shape when dropped on dish, it is ready to pour into pan.

Stir in vanilla and cherries. Scrape into greased 9 × 9 inch (22 × 22 cm) pan. Cool. Cut into squares.

Pictured on page 143.

BROWN SUGAR FUDGE

This sets up firmly and melts in your mouth when you eat it.

Brown sugar, packed	**2 cups**	**500 mL**
Granulated sugar	**1 cup**	**250 mL**
Corn syrup	**2 tbsp.**	**30 mL**
Butter or margarine	**2 tbsp.**	**30 mL**
Salt	**1/8 tsp.**	**0.5 mL**
Milk	**2/3 cup**	**150 mL**
Coconut or nuts	**1/2 cup**	**125 mL**

Measure first 6 ingredients into heavy saucepan. Stir often over medium heat until boiling. Boil without stirring until it reaches soft ball stage on candy thermometer, 235°F (113°C), or until a small spoonful forms a soft ball in cold water. Remove from heat.

Cool until you can almost hold your hand against the bottom of saucepan. Beat until it loses its glossy appearance and begins to thicken. Stir in coconut or nuts. Pour into greased 8 × 8 inch (20 × 20 cm) pan. Cool and cut into squares.

Note: If you miss the crucial point of pouring fudge just before it sets, it can be shaped into rolls and coated with crushed or finely chopped nuts. Slice to serve.

PEANUT BRITTLE

The easiest and the best.

Granulated sugar	2 cups	500 mL
Light corn syrup	1 cup	250 mL
Water	½ cup	125 mL
Butter or margarine	¼ cup	60 mL
Salted peanuts	2 cups	500 mL
Vanilla	1 tsp.	5 mL
Baking soda	2 tsp.	10 mL

Grease large baking sheet with sides and set aside.

Put sugar, syrup and water into large heavy saucepan. Bring to boil, stirring to dissolve sugar. Boil, stirring often, to soft ball stage, 235°F (112°C). In ice water it forms a ball which flattens easily.

Add peanuts and butter, stirring to mix. Continue boiling to hard crack stage, 300°F (150°C) or until a small amount dropped into ice water separates into threads which are hard and brittle. Stir frequently to prevent scorching.

Very quickly stir in vanilla and baking soda. Mixture will foam. Pour while still foaming onto greased baking sheet. Cool. To serve, break into small pieces. Makes about 2 pounds (900 g).

Pictured on page 143.

CURRIED PECANS

Good for eating at home or giving as a gift. Superb!

Pecans	2 cups	500 mL
Butter or margarine	1½ tbsp.	25 mL
Curry powder	1 tsp.	5 mL
Salt	½ tsp.	2 mL

Put pecans and butter into 9 × 9 inch (22 × 22 cm) pan. Heat in 350°F (180°C) oven until butter melts. Stir well to coat nuts. Continue to roast, stirring every 2 to 3 minutes for about 15 minutes. Remove from oven. Transfer to paper towels so grease will be absorbed a bit then put nuts into bowl.

Sprinkle with curry powder and salt. Stir to mix thoroughly. Makes 2 cups (500 mL).

Rich with fruit and spices. Makes a good wedding cake as well as a good Christmas cake.

Seedless raisins	2 lbs.	908 g
Seeded raisins	1 lb.	454 g
Currants	1 lb.	454 g
Dates, chopped	1 lb.	454 g
Cut candied mixed fruit	½ lb.	227 g
Candied cherries, halved	½ lb.	227 g
Blanched almonds, chopped	1½ cups	375 mL
Walnuts, chopped	1 cup	250 mL
All-purpose flour	2 cups	500 mL
Butter, softened	1 lb.	454 g
Brown sugar, packed	1½ cups	375 mL
Granulated sugar	1½ cups	375 mL
Eggs	12	12
Vanilla	1 tsp.	5 mL
Lemon, juice and grated rind	1	1
All-purpose flour	3 cups	650 mL
Baking soda	1 tsp.	5 mL
Cream of tartar	2 tsp.	10 mL
Cinnamon	2 tsp.	10 mL
Mace	1 tsp.	5 mL
Nutmeg	¼ tsp.	1 mL

Combine first 9 ingredients in large bowl. Stir to coat. Set aside.

Cream butter with both sugars. Beat in eggs gradually. Add remaining ingredients in order given. Mix well.

Add fruit mixture. Stir to mix. Line 3 greased 9 × 5 inch (22 × 13 cm) loaf pans and 1 pan 4 × 8 inch (10 × 20 cm) with greased brown paper. Spoon batter into pans. Bake in 275°F (140°C) oven for about 3 hours. Makes 3 regular cakes and 1 small cake.

Paré Pointer

We call him Buttons. He is always popping off at the wrong time.

WHITE FRUIT CAKE

This light colored cake is a great addition to any tray of goodies. Moist and pretty.

Golden raisins	2 cups	500 mL
Cut mixed peel	¾ cup	175 mL
Candied pineapple rings, diced	2	2
Slivered almonds	1 cup	250 mL
Candied cherries, halved	1 cup	250 mL
All-purpose flour	¾ cup	175 mL
Butter or margarine, softened	1½ cups	375 mL
Granulated sugar	1½ cups	375 mL
Eggs	6	6
Milk	¼ cup	60 mL
Vanilla	1 tsp.	5 mL
Almond flavoring	1 tsp.	5 mL
Lemon flavoring	½ tsp.	2 mL
All-purpose flour	3 cups	750 mL
Baking powder	1 tsp.	5 mL
Salt	½ tsp.	2 mL

Line 2 greased 6½ inch (16.5 cm) and 1 greased 5 inch (13 cm) round fruit cake pans with brown paper. Grease paper. Set aside.

Mix first 6 ingredients well to coat fruit with flour. Set aside.

Cream butter and sugar together well. Beat in eggs, 1 at a time. Mix in milk and flavorings.

Stir in flour, baking powder and salt. Add floured fruit. Mix. Spoon into prepared pans. Bake in 350°F (180°C) oven for 15 minutes. Turn oven to 300°F (150°C) for 1 hour, then turn oven to 275°F (140°C) until an inserted toothpick comes out clean. Total baking time is about 1¾ hours. Allow to ripen 3 to 4 weeks. Makes 2 medium cakes and 1 small cake.

Paré Pointer

If a little nut can hold its ground, it has a good chance of becoming a mighty oak.

Throughout this book measurements are given in conventional and metric measure. To compensate for differences between the two measurements due to rounding, a full metric measure is not always used.

The cup used is the standard 8 fluid ounce.

Temperature is given in degrees Fahrenheit and Celsius.

Baking pan measurements are in inches and centimetres, as well as quarts and litres. An exact conversion is given below as well as the working equivalent.

Spoons	Exact Conversion	Standard Metric Measure
¼ teaspoon	1.2 millilitres	1 millilitre
½ teaspoon	2.4 millilitres	2 millilitres
1 teaspoon	4.7 millilitres	5 millilitres
2 teaspoons	9.4 millilitres	10 millilitres
1 tablespoon	14.2 millilitres	15 millilitres

Cups		
¼ cup (4 T)	56.8 millilitres	50 millilitres
⅓ cup (5⅓ T)	75.6 millilitres	75 millilitres
½ cup (8 T)	113.7 millilitres	125 millilitres
⅔ cup (10⅔ T)	151.2 millilitres	150 millilitres
¾ cup (12 T)	170.5 millilitres	175 millilitres
1 cup (16 T)	227.3 millilitres	250 millilitres
4½ cups	984.8 millilitres	1000 millilitres, 1 litre

Ounces — Weight		
1 oz.	28.3 grams	30 grams
2 oz.	56.7 grams	55 grams
3 oz.	85 grams	85 grams
4 oz.	113.4 grams	125 grams
5 oz.	141.7 grams	140 grams
6 oz.	170.1 grams	170 grams
7 oz.	198.4 grams	200 grams
8 oz.	226.8 grams	250 grams
16 oz.	453.6 grams	500 grams
32 oz.	917.2 grams	1000 grams, 1 kg

Pans, Casseroles

8 × 8 inch, 20 × 20 cm, 2L	8 × 2 inch round, 20 × 5 cm, 2L
9 × 9 inch, 22 × 22 cm, 2.5L	9 × 2 inch round, 22 × 5 cm, 2.5L
9 × 13 inch, 22 × 33 cm, 4L	10 × 4½ inch tube, 25 × 11 cm, 5L
10 × 15 inch, 25 × 38 cm, 1.2L	8 × 4 × 3 inch loaf, 20 × 10 × 7 cm, 1.5L
11 × 17 inch, 28 × 43 cm, 1.5L	9 × 5 × 3 inch loaf, 23 × 12 × 7 cm, 2L

Oven Temperatures

Fahrenheit	Celsius	Fahrenheit	Celsius	Fahrenheit	Celsius
175°	80°	300°	150°	425°	220°
200°	100°	325°	160°	450°	230°
225°	110°	350°	180°	475°	240°
250°	120°	375°	190°	500°	260°
275°	140°	400°	200°		

INDEX

Company's Coming — Taste The Tradition

SAVE $5.00

Mail to:
COMPANY'S COMING PUBLISHING LIMITED
BOX 8037, STATION "F"
EDMONTON, ALBERTA, CANADA T6H 4N9

Please send the following number of **Company's Coming Cookbooks** to the address on the reverse side of this coupon:

Qty.	Title	Each	Total
	150 DELICIOUS SQUARES	$9.95	
	CASSEROLES	$9.95	
	MUFFINS & MORE	$9.95	
	SALADS	$9.95	
	APPETIZERS	$9.95	
	DESSERTS	$9.95	
	SOUPS & SANDWICHES	$9.95	
	HOLIDAY ENTERTAINING	$9.95	
	COOKIES	$9.95	
	VEGETABLES	$9.95	
	MAIN COURSES	$9.95	
	PASTA	$9.95	
	CAKES (September 1990)	$9.95	
	JEAN PARÉ'S FAVORITES VOLUME ONE 232 pages, hard cover	$17.95	

Total Qty.		
	Total Cost of Cookbooks	$
	Plus $1.00 postage and handling per copy	$
Less $5.00 for every third copy per order	—	$
Plus International Shipping Expenses (add $4.00 if outside Canada and U.S.A.)		$
Total Amount Enclosed		$

Special Mail Offer: Order any 2 **Company's Coming Cookbooks** by mail at regular prices and **save $5.00** on every third copy per order. Not valid in combination with any other offer.

Orders Outside Canada — amount enclosed must be paid in U.S. Funds.

Make cheque or money order payable to: "Company's Coming Publishing Limited

Prices subject to change after December 31, 1992.

Sorry, no C.O.D.'s.

GIVE  TO A FRIEND!

Please send Company's Coming Cookbooks listed on the reverse side of this coupon to:

NAME _____

STREET _____

CITY _____

PROVINCE/STATE _____ POSTAL CODE/ZIP _____

GIFT GIVING — WE MAKE IT EASY!

We will send Company's Coming cookbooks directly to the recipients of your choice — the perfect gift for birthdays, showers, Mother's Day, Father's Day, graduation or any occasion!

Please specify the number of copies of each title on the reverse side of this coupon and provide us with the name and address for each gift order. Enclose a personal note or card and we will include it with your order . . .

. . . and don't forget to take advantage of the **$5.00 saving** — buy 2 copies of **Company's Coming Cookbooks** by mail and **save $5.00** on every third copy per order.

Company's Coming — We Make It Easy — You Make it Delicious!

GIVE Company's Coming TO A FRIEND!

Please send Company's Coming Cookbooks listed on the reverse side of this coupon to:

NAME _____

STREET _____

CITY _____

PROVINCE/STATE _____ POSTAL CODE/ZIP _____

GIFT GIVING — WE MAKE IT EASY!

We will send Company's Coming cookbooks directly to the recipients of your choice — the perfect gift for birthdays, showers, Mother's Day, Father's Day, graduation or any occasion!

Please specify the number of copies of each title on the reverse side of this coupon and provide us with the name and address for each gift order. Enclose a personal note or card and we will include it with your order . . .

. . . and don't forget to take advantage of the **$5.00 saving** — buy 2 copies of **Company's Coming Cookbooks** by mail and **save $5.00** on every third copy per order.

Company's Coming — We Make It Easy — You Make it Delicious!

Company's Coming

Taste The Tradition

SAVE $5.00

Mail to:
COMPANY'S COMING PUBLISHING LIMITED
BOX 8037, STATION "F"
EDMONTON, ALBERTA, CANADA T6H 4N9

Please send the following number of **Company's Coming Cookbooks** to the address on the reverse side of this coupon:

Qty.	Title	Each	Total
	150 DELICIOUS SQUARES	$9.95	
	CASSEROLES	$9.95	
	MUFFINS & MORE	$9.95	
	SALADS	$9.95	
	APPETIZERS	$9.95	
	DESSERTS	$9.95	
	SOUPS & SANDWICHES	$9.95	
	HOLIDAY ENTERTAINING	$9.95	
	COOKIES	$9.95	
	VEGETABLES	$9.95	
	MAIN COURSES	$9.95	
	PASTA	$9.95	
	CAKES (September 1990)	$9.95	
	JEAN PARÉ'S FAVORITES **VOLUME ONE** 232 pages, hard cover	$17.95	

Total Qty.			
	Total Cost of Cookbooks	$	
	Plus $1.00 postage and handling per copy	$	
Less $5.00 for every third copy per order	— $		
Plus International Shipping Expenses (add $4.00 if outside Canada and U.S.A.)	$		
Total Amount Enclosed	$		

Special Mail Offer: Order any 2 **Company's Coming Cookbooks** by mail at regular prices and **save $5.00** on every third copy per order.
Not valid in combination with any other offer.

Orders Outside Canada — amount enclosed must be paid in U.S. Funds.

Make cheque or money order payable to: "Company's Coming Publishing Limited

Prices subject to change after December 31, 1992.

Sorry, no C.O.D.'s.

Company's Coming

Taste The Tradition

SAVE $5.00

Mail to:
COMPANY'S COMING PUBLISHING LIMITED
BOX 8037, STATION "F"
EDMONTON, ALBERTA, CANADA T6H 4N9

Please send the following number of **Company's Coming Cookbooks** to the address on the reverse side of this coupon:

Qty.	Title	Each	Total
	150 DELICIOUS SQUARES	$9.95	
	CASSEROLES	$9.95	
	MUFFINS & MORE	$9.95	
	SALADS	$9.95	
	APPETIZERS	$9.95	
	DESSERTS	$9.95	
	SOUPS & SANDWICHES	$9.95	
	HOLIDAY ENTERTAINING	$9.95	
	COOKIES	$9.95	
	VEGETABLES	$9.95	
	MAIN COURSES	$9.95	
	PASTA	$9.95	
	CAKES (September 1990)	$9.95	
	JEAN PARÉ'S FAVORITES **VOLUME ONE** 232 pages, hard cover	$17.95	

Total Qty.			
	Total Cost of Cookbooks	$	
	Plus $1.00 postage and handling per copy	$	
Less $5.00 for every third copy per order	— $		
Plus International Shipping Expenses (add $4.00 if outside Canada and U.S.A.)	$		
Total Amount Enclosed	$		

Special Mail Offer: Order any 2 **Company's Coming Cookbooks** by mail at regular prices and **save $5.00** on every third copy per order.
Not valid in combination with any other offer.

Orders Outside Canada — amount enclosed must be paid in U.S. Funds.

Make cheque or money order payable to: "Company's Coming Publishing Limited

Prices subject to change after December 31, 1992.

Sorry, no C.O.D.'s.

GIVE  TO A FRIEND!

Please send Company's Coming Cookbooks listed on the reverse side of this coupon to:

NAME _____

STREET _____

CITY _____

PROVINCE/STATE _____ POSTAL CODE/ZIP _____

GIFT GIVING — WE MAKE IT EASY!

We will send Company's Coming cookbooks directly to the recipients of your choice — the perfect gift for birthdays, showers, Mother's Day, Father's Day, graduation or any occasion!

Please specify the number of copies of each title on the reverse side of this coupon and provide us with the name and address for each gift order. Enclose a personal note or card and we will include it with your order . . .

. . . and don't forget to take advantage of the **$5.00 saving** — buy 2 copies of **Company's Coming Cookbooks** by mail and **save $5.00** on every third copy per order.

Company's Coming — We Make It Easy — You Make it Delicious!

GIVE *Company's Coming* TO A FRIEND!

Please send Company's Coming Cookbooks listed on the reverse side of this coupon to:

NAME _____

STREET _____

CITY _____

PROVINCE/STATE _____ POSTAL CODE/ZIP _____

GIFT GIVING — WE MAKE IT EASY!

We will send Company's Coming cookbooks directly to the recipients of your choice — the perfect gift for birthdays, showers, Mother's Day, Father's Day, graduation or any occasion!

Please specify the number of copies of each title on the reverse side of this coupon and provide us with the name and address for each gift order. Enclose a personal note or card and we will include it with your order . . .

. . . and don't forget to take advantage of the **$5.00 saving** — buy 2 copies of **Company's Coming Cookbooks** by mail and **save $5.00** on every third copy per order.

Company's Coming — We Make It Easy — You Make it Delicious!

It isn't wise to have helpers to make these. Too many disappear along the way.

Pecans	1 lb.	450 g
Corn syrup	1½ cups	375 mL
Butter or margarine	1 cup	250 mL
Brown sugar packed	1 cup	250 mL
Sweetened condensed milk	1 cup	250 mL
Semisweet chocolate chips	2 cups	500 mL
Butter or margarine	¼ cup	60 mL
Parowax	½ bar	½ bar

Spread pecans over bottom of greased 9 × 13 inch (22 × 33 cm) and 8 × 8 inch (20 × 20 cm) pans.

Combine syrup, first amount of butter, sugar and condensed milk in heavy saucepan. Bring to a boil stirring. Continue to boil slowly over low heat, stirring often, for about 25 minutes to medium-hard stage 250°F (120°C). A small amount dropped in ice water will form a firm ball that will hold its shape but can easily be flattened. Pour over pecans. Cool. Cover large pan or tray with plastic wrap. Spoon out pecan mixture in small clumps. Freeze until firm for easy dipping.

Melt chocolate chips, second amount of butter and wax together in small saucepan. Dip pecan clumps. Place on plastic wrap or waxed paper to set. Makes about 5 dozen.

Note: Wax used measures 2½ × 2½ × ⅝ inches (6.5 × 6.5 × 1.5 cm).

FOOTBALL PÂTÉ

This quick pâté is a blessing to busy holidayers. The flavor is excellent. Make the day before.

Butter or margarine	**⅓ cup**	**75 mL**
Chopped fresh mushrooms	**2 cups**	**500 mL**
Chopped onion	**1 cup**	**250 mL**
Canned liverwurst spread or liverwurst sausage	**24 oz.**	**750 g**
Brandy flavoring	**1 tsp.**	**5 mL**
Onion powder	**½ tsp.**	**2 mL**
Peppercorns and pimiento		

Melt butter in frying pan. Add mushrooms and onion. Sauté until onions are clear and soft, and mixture is fairly dry of moisture.

Stir in next 3 ingredients. Put into bowl. Chill. Remove from bowl. Shape into football. Place on tray. Cover and chill until needed.

Garnish with peppercorns and strips of pimiento to resemble a football. Serve with crackers.

CURRY DIP

Indulge in this easy and speedy dip. Curry flavor is mild and adds to the good taste.

Mayonnaise	**1 cup**	**250 mL**
Grated onion	**2 tsp.**	**10 mL**
Horseradish	**2 tsp.**	**10 mL**
Curry powder	**1 tsp.**	**5 mL**
Salt	**1 tsp.**	**5 mL**
Fresh vegetables, cut up		

Mix first 5 ingredients together. Serve with assorted vegetables, mushrooms, broccoli, pepper rings, cauliflower, etc. Makes approximately 1 cup (250 mL).

A tantalizing aroma fills the air when these are cooking. Makes a super special finger food, soft and tender to eat.

Spareribs, cut short	3½ lbs.	1.5 kg
Water to cover		
Soy sauce	½ cup	125 mL
Apple juice	1 cup	250 mL
Red wine vinegar	2 tbsp.	30 mL
Ginger powder	1 tsp.	5 mL
Garlic powder	½ tsp.	2 mL
Drops of hot pepper sauce	5	5
All-purpose flour		
Fat for deep-frying		

Cut ribs apart and put into large pot. Cover with water. Bring to a boil. Simmer, covered, for 30 minutes until partially cooked. Drain.

Put soy sauce, apple juice, vinegar, ginger, garlic powder and pepper sauce into bowl. Stir well. Add ribs. Cover and chill several hours or overnight, turning bowl occasionally to allow for complete coverage of marinade.

Drain well. Dredge ribs in flour. Deep-fry in hot fat 375°F (190°C) until browned. Drain on paper towels. Serve hot or cold. Serves 8.

Paré Pointer

She thinks a football coach has four wheels.

STUFFED MUSHROOMS

Among the best finger food snacks. Use smaller mushrooms if desired.

Large mushrooms	12	12
Mushroom stems	12	12
Dry bread crumbs	1/4 cup	50 mL
Finely chopped pecans or walnuts	1/2 cup	125 mL
Butter or margarine, melted	1/4 cup	50 mL
Garlic powder	1/4 tsp.	1 mL
Thyme	1/4 tsp.	1 mL

Sliced green onions for garnish
Chopped fresh parsley for garnish

Gently twist stems out of mushrooms. Set mushroom caps aside.

Chop mushroom stems fairly fine. Mix with crumbs, nuts, butter, garlic powder and thyme. Stuff mushrooms. Arrange on baking pan.

Garnish each with green onion or parsley. Bake in 350°F (180°C) oven for about 20 minutes.

HORSERADISH SAUCE

Instead of the usual plain horseradish, set this beside the beef.

Mayonnaise	1 cup	250 mL
Sour cream	1/2 cup	125 mL
Finely chopped green onion	2 tbsp.	30 mL
Horseradish	1 1/2 tbsp.	25 mL
Salt	1/2 tsp.	2 mL
Pepper	1/8 tsp.	0.5 mL

Measure all ingredients into small bowl. Mix together to blend. Serve with hot or cold beef. Makes 1 1/2 cups (375 mL).

BARON OF BEEF

All football enthusiasts will be clamoring for the outside cut.

Standing rib roast, boned and rolled	4½ lbs.	2 kg
Cajun seasoning		
Large buns, split and buttered		

Have meat at room temperature for about ½ hour. Sprinkle with seasoning and rub in well over outer surface. Place in roasting pan. Roast uncovered in 325°F (170°C) oven for 2½ to 3½ hours depend–ing on degree of doneness preferred. Place on cutting board on tray in prominent spot on buffet table. Supply ketchup, Horseradish Sauce, page 22, mustard, relish, salt and pepper. Serves 8 generously.

CAJUN SEASONING

Salt	3 tsp.	15 mL
Cayenne pepper	¼ tsp.	1 mL
Pepper	⅛ tsp.	0.5 mL
Garlic powder	⅛ tsp.	0.5 mL
Chili powder	⅛ tsp.	0.5 mL

Mix all ingredients together well. Rub into outer roast beef before cooking.

CUCUMBER SALAD

A mild creamy salad.

Medium onion, thinly sliced	1	1
Cold water to cover		
Sour cream	1 cup	250 mL
White vinegar	2 tbsp.	30 mL
Granulated sugar	4 tsp.	20 mL
Salt	2 tsp.	10 mL
Pepper	¼ tsp.	1 mL
Medium cucumbers, peeled and sliced	2	2

Cover sliced onion with water. Let stand 1 hour. Drain very well.

Combine sour cream, vinegar, sugar, salt and pepper.

Add cucumber slices and onion. Stir. Chill 2 or 3 hours before serving. Makes 4 cups (1 L).

VALENTINE'S DAY

If food is the language of love, this is the perfect day for a romantic dinner for two. Served by candlelight, this is a meal to remember.

This is a day for ruffles and lace. If you have silver, crystal and china, use them. Pink and white or red and white decorations are in order, as are tea roses or sweetheart roses. Decorate with Cupids, arrows and streamers.

Valentine's Day can also mean more than two for dinner. When gathering with friends, drink a toast to everyone in love. Then you might like to toast everyone who has ever been in love ... and perhaps everyone who hopes to be in love. When inviting several guests, pin a red paper heart on each guest's sleeve or have hearts attached to arm bands. It's the night to wear your heart on your sleeve.

For children or teens, try placing a heart shaped box in the center of the table with a ribbon going from the box to each plate. Attach one person's name to the end of each ribbon contained in the box. The person seated by each plate will then pull the ribbon to choose a partner for games. Another idea is to have either the boys or the girls choose their seats, then each pull a ribbon to see who will sit beside them.

Heart-shaped cookies are always welcome as are valentine candies with their sweet little quotes. Add romantic music for that finishing touch and your party will say "Be My Valentine".

MENU

Pink Champagne
or
Mock Champagne
Cupid's Dip

Spinach Tomato Salad

Beef Bourguignon
Parslied Rice
Stuffed Zucchini
Have A Heart Salad

Strawberry Cheesecake

MOCK CHAMPAGNE

A sparkling punch that can easily be turned into a single sparkling drink. Just use equal quantities of cider and ginger ale.

Apple cider	2 qts.	2 L
Ginger ale	2 qts.	2 L
Grenadine syrup (optional)		

Pour cider and ginger ale into punch bowl. Add enough grenadine to make a light pink color. Serve with ice cubes in each glass. Makes 4 quarts (4 L).

CUPID'S DIP

When the ancient Romans fed grapes to their loved ones, they didn't have a dip like this to enjoy along with them.

Granulated sugar	1/4 cup	60 mL
Cornstarch	1/4 cup	60 mL
Salt	1/4 tsp.	1 mL
Pineapple juice	1 cup	250 mL
Orange juice	1/4 cup	50 mL
Lemon juice	2 tbsp.	30 mL
Eggs, beaten	2	2
Grenadine syrup	2 tbsp.	30 mL
Cream cheese, softened	8 oz.	250 g

Assorted fruit: grapes, melon, apple
slices, orange sections, banana,
cherries, strawberries

Mix sugar, cornstarch and salt in saucepan.

Add pineapple, orange and lemon juices. Heat and stir in eggs and grenadine until it boils and thickens.

Add cheese in small pieces. Whisk or beat until melted and smooth. Chill. Serve with fruit. Makes 3 cups (750 mL).

SPINACH TOMATO SALAD

Very colorful with a just–the–right–nip dressing.

DRESSING

Mayonnaise	1 tbsp.	15 mL
Salad oil	1½ tsp.	7 mL
Red wine vinegar	1½ tsp.	7 mL
Granulated sugar	½ tsp.	2 mL
Salt	⅛ tsp.	0.5 mL
Pepper sprinkle		
Garlic powder, light sprinkle		

Mix all ingredients together well. Makes a scant 2 tbsp. (30 mL).

SALAD

Spinach leaves, handful	1	1
Fresh sliced mushrooms	¼ cup	50 mL
Cherry tomatoes, quartered	2	2
Hard boiled egg	1	1
Grated Parmesan cheese		

In large bowl put spinach leaves, mushrooms and tomatoes. Add ¾ of the dressing. Toss lightly and arrange on 2 salad plates. Have a few tomato slices showing on top.

Cut eggs in half lengthwise. With clean sharp knife cut each half into 3 long wedges. Divide among plates placing along side of spinach. Drizzle remaining dressing over all. Sprinkle with Parmesan cheese. Serves 2.

Pictured on page 35.

ROMAINE TOMATO SALAD: Use Romaine lettuce instead of spin–ach leaves.

He found the best way to see flying saucers was to pinch a waitress.

BEEF BOURGUIGNON

An extra special dish that is economical as well. In heart shaped pastry, it has Cupid's seal of approval.

All-purpose flour	2 tbsp.	30 mL
Salt	¾ tsp.	3 mL
Pepper	¼ tsp.	1 mL
Round steak or stew meat, cut into 1 inch (2.5 cm) squares or cubes	1 lb.	450 g
Cooking oil	1 tbsp.	15 mL
Chopped onion	¾ cup	175 mL
Burgundy or other red wine	1 cup	250 mL
Beef stock	½ cup	125 mL
Medium carrot, diced	1	1
Garlic clove, minced	½	½
Parsley flakes	½ tsp.	2 mL
Bay leaf, small	½	½
Thyme	⅛ tsp.	0.5 mL
Canned mushroom pieces, drained (½ of 10 oz., 284 mL)	5 oz.	142 mL
Frozen puff pastry, thawed		

Mix flour, salt and pepper together in bag.

Drop in a few pieces of meat. Shake to coat. Brown in oil in frying pan. Repeat with rest of meat, browning a few pieces at a time, adding more oil as needed. Transfer browned meat to 2 quart (2 L) casserole.

Brown onion in frying pan, adding more oil if necessary. Add to casserole.

Add wine, beef stock, carrot, garlic, parsley, bay leaf and thyme. Mix thoroughly. Cover and bake in 325°F (160°C) oven for 2½ hours. Discard bay leaf.

Add mushrooms. Mix lightly. Continue to bake until mushrooms are heated through and meat is tender. Cool.

Roll puff pastry to fit 3 individual heart shaped pans. Spoon meat mixture into shell. Dampen rim. Cover with rolled out pastry. Press to seal edge. Cut slits in top. Bake in 400°F (200°C) oven until browned and puffed, about 20 minutes. Invert on small plate and invert again on dinner plate so it will be right side up. Makes 3 individual meat pies.

Pictured on page 35.

PARSLIED RICE

Light fluffy rice is always popular.

Long grain rice	1½ cups	375 mL
Water	3 cups	750 mL
Salt	¾ tsp.	4 mL
Butter or margarine	3 tbsp.	50 mL
Parsley flakes	2 tsp.	10 mL

Combine rice, water and salt in saucepan. Bring to a boil, stirring occasionally. Boil slowly, covered, for about 15 minutes. All water should be absorbed.

Add butter and parsley. Fluff with fork. Makes about 4½ cups (1 L). Serves 8.

Pictured on page 35.

HAVE A HEART SALAD

Pass the plate and have a heart.

Strawberry flavored gelatin	3 oz.	85 g
Boiling water	1 cup	225 mL
Applesauce	½ cup	125 mL
Mayonnaise	¼ cup	50 mL
Whipping cream	½ cup	125 mL
Jellied red hearts		
Mayonnaise, tinted pink		

Dissolve gelatin in boiling water in bowl.

Add applesauce. Whisk in mayonnaise. Chill until the consistency of syrup.

Beat cream until stiff. Fold into thickened jelly. Spoon into small individual heart shaped molds. Chill. Unmold on lettuce lined plates. Top with Jellied Hearts, page 29. Pipe with pink-tinted mayonnaise. Makes 4 to 5 hearts. Double recipe to make 8.

Pictured on page 35.

(continued on next page)

JELLIED HEARTS: Dissolve 3 oz. (85 g) pkg. strawberry flavored gelatin in ½ cup (125 mL) boiling water. Pour into 9 × 5 inch (22 × 13 cm) loaf pan. Chill well. Cut into hearts.

STUFFED ZUCCHINI

A basket filled with vegetables. Very showy.

Zucchini, 6 inch (15 cm)	2	2
Diced carrot	¼ cup	50 mL
Peas, frozen or fresh	¼ cup	50 mL
Pinch of garlic powder		
Dry bread crumbs	½ cup	125 mL
Fresh tomatoes peeled, diced	¼ cup	50 mL
Poultry seasoning	⅛ tsp.	0.5 mL
Parsley flakes	¼ tsp.	1 mL
Salt	⅛ tsp.	0.5 mL
Pinch of pepper		
Water	1 tbsp.	15 mL
Grated Cheddar cheese	2 tbsp.	30 mL

Cut unpeeled zucchini in half lengthwise. Boil in salted water for 5 minutes. Drain. Scoop out seeds and some of the pulp. Discard or use for another purpose.

Cook carrot, peas and garlic in small amount of salted water until tender. Drain.

Mix crumbs, tomatoes, poultry seasoning, parsley flakes, salt and pepper together. Stir in water. Add to carrot and peas. Stir. Stuff zucchini shells.

Sprinkle with cheese. Bake in 350°F (180°C) oven for 20 minutes or until heated through. Makes 1¼ cups (300 mL) stuffing. Serves 2.

Note: To peel tomatoes plunge into boiling water for about 1 minute. Peel and cool.

Pictured on page 35.

CHOCOLATE HEARTS

Although this is a fancy extra to make, it adds that special something.

Semisweet chocolate squares	**4 x 1 oz.**	**4 x 28 g**
Parowax	**¼ bar**	**¼ bar**

Cut chocolate and wax into chunks for easier melting. Put in top of double boiler over hot water (not boiling) to melt. Spread on waxed paper lined pan ⅛ inch (3 mm) thick. Chill until not quite as firm as original chocolate. Cut into hearts or other desired shapes, leaving all in pan. Chill until firm. Carefully remove hearts from paper. Makes 16 hearts 1½ × 1 inch (3.75 × 2.5 cm).

CHOCOLATE LEAVES: Choose matching or different leaves from nontoxic plants. Wash and pat dry. Paint backs of leaves with brush or knife, covering leaf with ⅛ inch (3 mm) layer of chocolate. Be careful not to get any chocolate on other side. Lay coated leaves on plate. Chill until firm. Carefully peel leaves off chocolate.

Note: Parowax measures approximately 1⅛ × 2½ × ⅝ inches thick (6 × 12.5 × 3 cm).

COOKIE HEARTS: Make Sugar Cookies, page 111. Cut out heart shaped cookies. Color granulated sugar by putting it in a small container with some red food coloring. Shake well. Sprinkle over cookies before baking. Cookies are especially nice when iced with pink or white butter frosting.

The reason a man's hair turns grey before his moustache is because his hair is much older of course.

STRAWBERRY CHEESECAKE

A scrumptious refrigerator dessert.

CRUST

Butter or margarine	¼ cup	60 mL
Graham cracker crumbs	1 cup	250 mL
Granulated sugar	2 tbsp.	30 mL
Cocoa	2 tbsp.	30 mL

FILLING

Strawberry flavored gelatin	3 oz.	85 g
Unflavored gelatin powder	¼ oz.	7 g
Boiling water	1 cup	225 mL
Frozen sliced strawberries, partly thawed	15 oz.	425 g
Cream cheese, softened	8 oz.	250 g
Icing (confectioner's) sugar	⅔ cup	150 mL
Whipping cream (or 2 env. topping)	2 cups	500 mL

Chocolate hearts for garnish
Whipped cream for garnish

Crust: Melt butter in saucepan. Stir in crumbs, sugar and cocoa. Measure ½ cup (125 mL) for topping. Press remaining crumbs into ungreased 9 inch (22 cm) springform pan. Bake in 350°F (180°C) oven for 10 minutes. Cool.

Filling: Mix both gelatin powders together well in bowl. Add water. Stir to dissolve. Mix in strawberries. Chill until syrupy.

Beat cream cheese and icing sugar together until fluffy.

Whip cream until stiff. Fold into cheese mixture. Fold into thickened jelly. Pour over crust. Sprinkle with reserved crumbs. Chill well. Cuts into 10 to 12 pieces.

Decorate with Chocolate Hearts, page 30, and whipped cream if desired.

Pictured on page 35.

Paré Pointer

It's nothing new that women want mens' wages. Haven't they always?

STUFFED BREASTS OF CHICKEN

Gourmet style which is easy to do and so attractive to serve.

Boneless chicken breasts	2	2
Butter or margarine	2 tbsp.	30 mL
Chopped onion	2 tbsp.	30 mL
Chopped celery	2 tbsp.	30 mL
Dry bread crumbs	1 cup	250 mL
Chives	1 tbsp.	15 mL
Poultry seasoning	1/4 tsp.	1 mL
Salt	1/16 tsp.	0.5 mL
Pepper sprinkle		
Milk	1 1/2 tbsp.	25 mL

Remove skin from chicken breast.

Melt butter in saucepan or frying pan. Add onion and celery. Sauté until onion is soft and clear. Remove from heat.

Add bread crumbs, chives, poultry seasoning, salt and pepper. Stir well to mix. Add more milk if needed to make dressing cling together. Divide between breasts to make a mound along the center length. Close and secure with picks. Place in baking dish. Spoon some Marmalade Orange Sauce over top. Bake uncovered in 325°F (160°C) oven until tender, about 45 minutes. Slice and arrange on plates. Spoon additional sauce over slices. Serves 2 generously.

MARMALADE ORANGE SAUCE

Orange marmalade	1/2 cup	125 mL
Concentrated orange juice	1 tbsp.	15 mL

Stir marmalade and concentrated juice together in saucepan over low heat. Spoon some over chicken breasts to bake. Spoon rest of sauce over top before serving.

Pictured on cover.

Paré Pointer

She thought a nightmare was a dark horse.

A three layered gorgeous dessert.

CRUST

All-purpose flour	1¼ cups	350 mL
Granulated sugar	2 tbsp.	30 mL
Butter or margarine, softened	¾ cup	175 mL

FILLING

Raspberry flavored gelatin	3 oz.	85 g
Boiling water	1 cup	225 mL
Frozen raspberries, partly thawed	15 oz.	425 g
Large white marshmallows	16	16
Sour cream	½ cup	125 mL
Grenadine syrup	1 tbsp.	15 mL
Whipping cream (or 1 env. topping)	1 cup	250 mL

Crust: Mix flour, sugar and butter together until crumbly. Press into ungreased 9 × 9 inch (22 × 22 cm) pan. Bake in 350°F (180°C) oven for 20 minutes. Cool.

Filling: Dissolve gelatin in boiling water in bowl. Add raspberries. Chill until syrupy. Pour over crumb crust. Chill.

Melt marshmallows in sour cream and grenadine in double boiler. Cool.

Whip cream until stiff. Fold into cooled marshmallow mixture. Spread over raspberry layer. Chill. Cuts into 9 pieces.

Pictured on cover.

For the cover photo, this dessert was prepared in a 9 inch (22 cm) springform pan using 2 raspberry layers and 2 marshmallow layers.

Pare Pointer

Aged comedians eventually end up in the old jokes home.

BROCCOLI RICE STIR FRY

Prepare wild rice early in the day. Add to the broccoli mixture to heat through. Add an extra dish of white rice, noodles or potatoes if you like, depending on your preference.

Wild rice	¼ cup	60 mL
Water	1 cup	250 mL
Salt	⅛ tsp.	0.5 mL
Broccoli flowerettes and peeled cut stems	1 cup	250 mL
Small red pepper, cut up	¼	¼
Celery ribs, cut into matchsticks	1	1
Carrots, cut into matchsticks	½	½
Green onion, sliced	1	1
Lemon juice	1½ tsp.	7 mL
Cooking oil	2 tsp.	10 mL

Cover rice with water, swish it around and drain through sieve. Rinse a second time. Cover rice with water and soak for 2 hours. Drain. Put rice, 4 cups (1 L) water and salt into saucepan. Bring to boil. Simmer, covered, for about 50 to 60 minutes until grains burst. Cool.

Put broccoli flowerettes and stems into large wok or frying pan over medium-high heat. Add remaining ingredients along with cooked wild rice. Add only part of the rice if you like the look of it better. Stir continually until vegetables are tender-crisp, about 3 to 5 minutes. Serves 2.

Pictured on cover.

VALENTINE'S DAY

ST. PATRICK'S DAY

A gay light-hearted day brimming with happy greetings. 'Tis the time for the wearing o' the green, eating green food and drinking green drinks! A day meant for a party. An Irish party, that is.

Decorate your table by using Irish motif table napkins and placemats. If you feel creative, a Leprechaun and mushroom centerpiece will help set the mood. And of course, have green shamrocks everywhere.

Some of the old Irish musical favorites are a must; "When Irish Eyes Are Smiling", "My Wild Irish Rose" and "Sweet Rosie O'Grady" are just a few. And don't forget to end the evening with a rousing rendition of "Take Me Home Again Kathleen". Will we ever find out who threw the overalls in Mrs. Murphy's chowder?

Irish or not — have an Irish party and you will find the luck o' the Irish will be yours — no blarney!

MENU

Margarita Slush
Frothy Lime Punch

Dill Dip with Green Vegetables
Stuffed Mushrooms

Corned Beef And Cabbage

Champ
Buttered Carrots

Mixed Salad
Lime Mold
Irish Soda Brown Bread

Key Lime Pie
Irish Coffee

MARGARITA SLUSH

To the health of the Irish!

Frozen lime juice, thawed	12 oz.	340 mL
Water	1½ cups	375 mL
Tequila	1½ cups	375 mL

Put all ingredients into plastic container. Put lid on tightly and shake. Put in freezer for 3 hours. Salt rims of glasses and fill. Serve with lemon or lime wedge. Makes about 36 oz. (1 L).

Note: To salt rims rub lip edge of glass with lemon or lime wedge. Dip glass into salt. To salt rims of several glasses, pour lemon juice into fruit nappie and have salt ready for dipping in another fruit nappie.

FROTHY LIME PUNCH

A delight to the eye as well as the palate. No Irish spirits in this!

Pineapple juice	8 cups	2 L
Lime drink mix (see note)	2 env.	2 env.
Granulated sugar	2 cups	450 mL
Lime sherbet	1 qt.	1 L
Seven Up or ginger ale	8 cups	2 L

Whole strawberries for garnish

Put pineapple juice and lime drink mix into punch bowl. Stir until sugar dissolves.

Spoon sherbet into punch bowl. Add Seven Up slowly. Let stand 15 minutes.

Add a few whole strawberries and serve. Makes about 20 cups (5 L).

Note: Lime drink mix (such as Kool-Aid) comes in envelopes to make 2 quarts (2 L) of liquid when used with water. Presweetened mix may be used. Just omit sugar. Lemon-lime flavor may be used if lime isn't available.

CHEESE STUFFED MUSHROOMS

A favorite of the leprechauns. And no wonder!

Large mushrooms	12	12
Cream cheese, softened	4 oz.	125 g
Sour cream	4 tsp.	20 mL
Dried chives	2 tsp.	10 mL
Seasoned salt	½ tsp.	2 mL
Bacon slices, partly cooked, halved	6	6

Twist stems from mushrooms. Reserve for another use.

Mix cream cheese, sour cream, chives and salt together. Spoon into mushrooms.

Cover mushrooms with bacon. Tuck ends underneath. Arrange in baking pan. Bake in 350°F (180°C) oven for about 20 minutes, or broil until sizzling hot. Arrange 3 mushrooms on each plate as a first course. Serves 4 leprechauns.

DILL DIP

A handy snack. Set out dip and chips for snackers to help themselves.

Mayonnaise	1 cup	250 mL
Sour cream	1 cup	250 mL
Parsley flakes	1 tsp.	5 mL
Dried dill weed	1 tsp.	5 mL
Beau Monde seasoning	1 tsp.	5 mL

Mix all ingredients together. Chill until needed. Serve with potato chips. Also good as a dip for raw vegetables. Makes 2 cups (500 mL).

Note: If Beau Monde seasoning isn't available, use ½ tsp. (2 mL) each of onion powder and celery salt.

CORNED BEEF AND CABBAGE

Even if your name isn't Dinty Moore, you will enjoy this old time dish.

Corned beef brisket	4 lbs.	1.8 kg
Water to cover		
Large onion, sliced	1	1
Whole cloves	3	3
Granulated sugar (optional)	¼ cup	50 mL
Garlic powder	¼ tsp.	1 mL
Medium to large cabbage, cut into wedges	1	1

Cover corned beef with water in large pot. Add onion, cloves, sugar and garlic powder. Bring to a boil. Cover and simmer until fork tender. This will take about 4 hours.

Remove meat and keep hot. Add cabbage wedges to pot. Cover and simmer 15 to 20 minutes until cabbage is cooked. Slice meat and arrange down center of platter. With slotted spoon, lift cabbage onto platter along sides of meat. Serves 8 to 10.

BUTTERED CARROTS

Bright, colorful, tasty. A perfect compliment for Corned Beef and Cabbage, above.

Medium carrots	12	12
Salted water		
Butter or margarine	4 tsp.	20 mL
Chives	2 tsp.	10 mL
Granulated sugar	1 tsp.	5 mL
Pepper sprinkle		

Cut carrots into bite size pieces. Cook in small amount of salted water until tender. Drain.

Add butter, chives, sugar and pepper. Stir lightly to mix well and to coat carrots. Serves 8.

This potato dish is mashed with green onion before a well is formed. Then melted butter added to the well completes the ever favorite potato treat.

Medium potatoes	**6**	**6**
Salted water		
Milk	**1 cup**	**250 mL**
Green onions, chopped	**8**	**8**
Butter or margarine	**¼ cup**	**50 mL**
Salt	**½ tsp.**	**2 mL**
Pepper	**⅛ tsp.**	**0.5 mL**
Butter, melted for garnish	**¼ cup**	**50 mL**

Boil peeled potatoes in small amount of salted water until tender. Drain. Mash.

Boil milk, onion, butter, salt and pepper together slowly for 2 minutes. Add to potatoes. Mash well. Taste for salt and pepper, adding more if needed. Spoon into flat shallow bowl. With spoon, smooth center and form a ridge around outside edge. Pour melted butter into potato center. Serves 4. Double recipe to serve 8.

LIME MOLD

Shimmering green salad with bits of cheese showing through. Quite a clear looking salad.

Lime flavored gelatin	**6 oz.**	**170 g**
Boiling water	**2½ cups**	**575 mL**
Crushed pineapple with juice	**14 oz.**	**398 mL**
Onion powder	**¼ tsp.**	**1 mL**
Grated Cheddar cheese	**1 cup**	**250 mL**

Dissolve gelatin in boiling water. Stir in pineapple and juice. Chill until syrupy.

Fold in cheese. Pour into 4 cup (900 mL) shamrock mold. Chill.

MIXED SALAD

An interesting mixture brought to life with a garlic, oil and vinegar dressing.

SALAD

Torn lettuce greens, pressed down	3 cups	750 mL
Grated Cheddar cheese	½ cup	125 mL
Avocado, peeled and cubed	1	1
Cut green beans, drained (or kidney beans)	14 oz.	398 mL
Tomato, cut up	1	1
Green onions, chopped	2	2
Croutons or shoestring potato chips or corn chips	1 cup	250 mL

Combine first 6 ingredients together in bowl. Toss with garlic dressing.

Sprinkle croutons over top. Serves 8.

GARLIC DRESSING

Cooking oil	½ cup	125 mL
Vinegar	¼ cup	50 mL
Granulated sugar	1 tsp.	5 mL
Garlic powder	½ tsp.	2 mL
Salt	2 tsp.	10 mL
Pepper	½ tsp.	2 mL
Dry mustard	½ tsp.	2 mL

Measure all ingredients into bowl. Whisk together. Pour over salad. Toss.

Pare Pointer

The Martian told the gas pump to take its finger out of its ear and listen!

IRISH SODA BROWN BREAD

'Tis an old staple still used even now. Try it toasted.

Whole wheat flour	4 cups	900 mL
All-purpose flour	1 cup	250 mL
Granulated sugar	2 tbsp.	30 mL
Baking soda	1½ tsp.	7 mL
Salt	1 tsp.	5 mL
Buttermilk	2⅓ cups	550 mL
Cooking oil	¼ cup	50 mL

Measure first 5 ingredients into large bowl. Mix together then make a well in center.

Add buttermilk and cooking oil. Stir just enough to moisten. Scrape into greased 9 × 5 × 3 inch (23 × 12 × 7 cm) loaf pan. Bake in 350°F (180°C) oven for about 1 hour. Remove from pan. Cool on rack. Serve plain or toasted with butter. Makes 1 loaf.

IRISH COFFEE

Now for an Irish finale.

Irish whiskey	1½ oz.	45 mL
Granulated sugar	1 tsp.	5 mL
Strong hot coffee		
Whipped cream		

Pour whiskey and sugar into Irish whiskey glass. Add coffee to ½ inch (1.25 cm) from top. Stir lightly. Pour on whipped cream, filling to the brim. Do not stir. Makes 1 serving.

Paré Pointer

Was it food containers that first did the can-can?

KEY LIME PIE

A delicate shade of green with a delectable flavor. Like biting into a cloud.

Unflavored gelatin powder	¼ oz.	7 g
Cold water	¼ cup	50 mL
Egg yolks	4	4
Granulated sugar	½ cup	125 mL
Lime juice	⅓ cup	75 mL
Salt	½ tsp.	2 mL
Grated lime peel	2 tsp.	10 mL
Green food coloring		
Egg whites	4	4
Granulated sugar	½ cup	125 mL
Whipping cream	1 cup	250 mL
Baked pie shell, 9 inch (22 cm)	1	1
Whipped cream for garnish		

Sprinkle gelatin over cold water in saucepan. Let stand 5 minutes.

Add egg yolks. Beat well. Add first amount of sugar, lime juice, salt, lime peel. Beat to mix. Tint a pale green. Heat and stir until boiling then remove from heat. Chill until mixture will leave a mound when spooned.

Beat egg whites until soft peaks form. Add second amount of sugar gradually while continuing to beat until stiff peaks form. Fold gelatin mixture into egg whites.

Beat cream until stiff. Fold into filling.

Turn into pie shell. Chill well. Garnish with additional whipped cream. Serves 6 generously.

Pare Pointer

Bakers make the best baseball pitchers because they know their batter.

Easter is one of the holiest days in the Christian faith.

Easter also signals that spring is to begin. It is the time for the birth of animals and the time for new flowers and leafy trees. Even people begin sprouting as cheerful Easter bonnets begin to appear.

When decorating for your Easter party, use plenty of mauve, yellow and other pastel shades. Daisies, irises, violets and Easter lilies will happily adorn any table. Pussy willows are always welcome if available. Place colored eggs and candied eggs here and there and perhaps chocolate rabbits and chickens for decor — but be on guard for eager little fingers!

An Easter ham is traditional for many. The lamb may easily be interchanged with the New Year's ham. Try the Crown Roast of Lamb for a special treat.

MENU

Golden Punch

Plymouth Rocks
Salmon Mousse
Toast Cups

Crown Roast of Lamb
Mint Sauce

Potato Noisette
Glazed Parsnips
Peas and Pods
Candied Carrots

Cabbage Salad
Cheesy Salad Mold

Hot Cross Buns

Lemon Meringue Pie

GOLDEN PUNCH

A dark golden color. Tasty.

Pineapple juice	12 cups	2.7 L
Prepared orange juice	6 cups	1.3 L
Cranberry juice	5 cups	1.1 L
Frozen condensed orange juice	12 oz.	341 g
Ginger ale	36 oz.	1 L
Orange slices		

Combine juices in punch bowl.

Just before serving add ginger ale and orange slices. Serve over ice. Makes 24 cups (5.4 L).

PLYMOUTH ROCKS

These are such neat little tricks. Served hot or cold, they are very tasty.

Sausage meat	½ lb.	225 g
Pickled onions, well drained	28	28
All-purpose flour	2 tbsp.	30 mL
Egg, beaten	1	1
Dry bread crumbs, rolled finely	½ cup	125 mL
Fat for deep-frying		

Pat sausage meat into small flat portions. Dust onions with flour. Wrap each onion with meat. Dampen hands with cold water for easier handling.

Dip each sausage ball into egg, roll in crumbs, and deep-fry in 375°F (190°C) fat until well browned. Serve hot or cold. These may also be baked in greased pan in 450°F (225°C) oven for 20 minutes or until browned. Makes about 26 to 28.

SCOTCH EGGS: The same method is used to make these. You will need larger quantities of sausage meat to wrap around hard-boiled eggs.

SALMON MOUSSE

This is the best in any form.

Unflavored gelatin powders	2 x ¼ oz.	2 x 7 g
Water	½ cup	125 mL
Granulated sugar	2 tbsp.	30 mL
Lemon juice	2 tbsp.	30 mL
Onion flakes	4 tsp.	20 mL
Salt	½ tsp.	2 mL
Paprika	½ tsp.	2 mL
Juice from salmon		
Canned salmon, mashed	15 oz.	426 g
Chopped celery	1½ cups	375 mL
Mayonnaise	1 cup	250 mL

Sprinkle gelatin over water in small saucepan. Let stand 5 minutes. Heat and stir to dissolve.

Add next 6 ingredients. Stir. Chill until consistency of syrup.

Remove round bones and skin from salmon. Mash. Fold salmon, celery and mayonnaise into gelatin mixture. Pour into 4 cup (900 mL) mold. Chill well to set. Unmold and serve with Toast Cups, below, or crackers.

TOAST CUPS

These are so easy to make yet look so special.

White bread slices	12	12

Cut crusts from sandwich loaf bread. Cut each slice into 4 squares. Press into small ungreased muffin cups. A small empty muffin cup that holds 4 tsp. (20 mL) is a good size. Bake in 350°F (180°C) oven on bottom rack for about 15 minutes until corners are well browned. Turn pan over to remove toast cups. Cool completely. Store in plastic bag. To serve, fill with filling or pile cups around filling. Makes 48.

CROWN ROAST OF LAMB

A gourmet feast.

Crown lamb roast, containing 16 ribs
Salt and pepper

STUFFING		
Chopped onion	¼ **cup**	**50 mL**
Chopped celery	¼ **cup**	**50 mL**
Butter or margarine	¼ **cup**	**50 mL**
Dry bread crumbs	**4 cups**	**1 L**
Parsley flakes	**2 tsp.**	**10 mL**
Poultry seasoning	**1½ tsp.**	**7 mL**
Salt	½ **tsp.**	**2 mL**
Pepper	⅛ **tsp.**	**0.5 mL**
Water, up to	**1 cup**	**250 mL**

Sprinkle all surfaces of meat with salt and pepper. Place meat in roaster on rack, rib ends up. Roast uncovered (or cover if you prefer) in 325°F (160°C) oven for 1 hour.

Stuffing: Meanwhile, sauté onion and celery in butter until onion is clear and soft.

Mix crumbs, parsley, poultry seasoning, salt and pepper together in bowl. Add onion, celery and any butter left in pan. Stir in water until dressing will hold together when squeezed in hand. Using 2 thick-nesses of foil, shape over your fist. Place in center of roast, pushing foil against sides of meat to keep stuffing from falling into drippings. Pack with stuffing. Cover dressing in ribs with foil lid. Cook extra stuffing in separate container. Add ¼ cup (50 mL) butter or margarine and more water if too dry. Continue to roast lamb until the degree of readiness you prefer is reached. If top of stuffing is dry, drizzle with melted butter or margarine or put all stuffing into bowl and mix with a bit of water. Serve with mint sauce or mint jelly. Makes medium size servings of 4 ribs each for 4 people. Double recipe to serve 8.

Pictured on page 53.

GRAVY: Mix ½ cup (125 mL) each of drippings and all-purpose flour with ¾ tsp. (3 mL) salt and ⅛ tsp. (0.5 mL) pepper. Stir in drippings (without fat) and water to measure 4 cups (1 L). Heat and stir to boil and thicken. Makes 4 cups (1 L).

MINT SAUCE

This is made from dried mint leaves. Serve with lamb.

Dried mint leaves, crumbled	1 tbsp.	15 mL
Boiling water	¼ cup	50 mL
Vinegar	2 tbsp.	30 mL
Granulated sugar	2 tsp.	10 mL

Put all 4 ingredients into small saucepan. Bring to a boil. Simmer about 2 minutes. Serve hot with lamb. Makes ⅓ cup (75 mL).

POTATO NOISETTE

Here are those tiny potatoes found in pricey restaurants.

Large potatoes	4	4
Salted water		
Butter or margarine	2 tbsp.	30 mL
Parsley flakes	1 tsp.	5 mL
Salt	¼ tsp.	1 mL
Pepper	⅛ tsp.	0.5 mL

Peel potatoes. With melon baller, scoop out 1 inch (2.5 cm) balls of potatoes. Boil in salted water 5 minutes. Drain. Pat dry with paper towels.

Melt butter in frying pan. Add potato balls. Cover and cook on medium heat for about 10 to 15 minutes until tender and browned.

Sprinkle with parsley, salt and pepper. Serves 4. Double recipe to serve 8.

Pictured on page 53.

Paré Pointer

Sometimes a wisecrack is an educated hole in the wall.

PEAS AND PODS

Make those peas extra special.

Frozen peas	10 oz.	284 g
Frozen Chinese pea pods	6 oz.	170 g
Granulated sugar	½ tsp.	2 mL
Salted water		
Butter or margarine	2 tbsp.	30 mL

Cook all peas and sugar together in salted water until done. Drain.

Add butter. Toss lightly to melt and coat peas. Serves 4 to 6. Double recipe to serve 8.

GLAZED PARSNIPS

Buttered and sugared, these are excellent.

Parsnips, cut into 2 inch (5 cm) lengths	2½ lbs.	1.1 kg
Salted water		
Butter or margarine	3 tbsp.	50 mL
Brown sugar	2 tbsp.	30 mL
Salt sprinkle		
Pepper sprinkle		

Cook parsnips in small amount of salted water until just tender. Don't overcook as they go mushy very easily. Drain.

Add remaining ingredients. Stir gently to melt butter and to coat parsnips. Makes 8 servings.

Pictured on page 53.

Rome was built at night because it wasn't built in a day.

CANDIED CARROTS

The glaze makes these shiny and irresistible.

Carrots cut in irregular shaped pieces	2 lbs.	1 kg
Salted water		
Butter or margarine	1 tbsp.	15 mL
All-purpose flour	2 tsp.	10 mL
Brown sugar	2 tbsp.	30 mL
Prepared orange juice	½ cup	125 mL

Cook carrots in small amount of salted water until tender. Drain.

Meanwhile, melt butter in small saucepan. Stir in flour and brown sugar. Add orange juice, stirring until mixture boils and thickens slightly. Pour over carrots. Stir to coat. Serves 8.

Pictured on page 53.

CHEESY SALAD MOLD

Unusual and good. Olives don't overpower other ingredients. A differ-ent combination of fruit, nuts and pickles. Crunchy.

Lemon flavored gelatin powder	3 oz.	85 g
Boiling water	1 cup	250 mL
Cold water (include juice from	1 cup	200 mL
pineapple)		
Whipping cream	½ cup	125 mL
Finely chopped nuts	½ cup	125 mL
Grated Cheddar cheese	1 cup	250 mL
Crushed pineapple drained	14 oz.	398 mL
Stuffed olives, sliced	½ cup	125 mL

Dissolve gelatin in boiling water. Add cold water. Chill to egg white consistency. Beat until fluffy.

Whip cream until stiff. Fold in nuts, cheese, pineapple and olives. Fold this mixture into gelatin. Pour into pretty serving bowl or into 4 cup (900 mL) mold. Serves 8 to 10.

CABBAGE SALAD

Careful, or your guests will make a meal of this.

SALAD

Shredded cabbage, pressed down	4 cups	1 L
Medium carrot, grated	1	1
Green onions, sliced	4 - 6	4 - 6
Sesame seeds, toasted in 350°F (180°C) oven for 5 to 8 minutes	2 tbsp.	30 mL
Instant chicken noodles, crumbled (see note)	3½ oz.	100 g

DRESSING

Package of noodle seasoning	1	1
Salad oil	½ cup	125 mL
Vinegar	3 tbsp.	50 mL
Granulated sugar	1 tbsp.	15 mL
Salt	1 tsp.	5 mL
Pepper	½ tsp.	2 mL

Salad: Combine salad ingredients in large bowl. If assembling ahead of time, keep out noodles and add later along with dressing.

Dressing: Mix all ingredients together. Pour over salad. Toss to mix. Serves 8 generously.

Note: Instant chicken noodles are found in the soup section of grocery stores. There are Japanese, Chinese and other brands.

EASTER

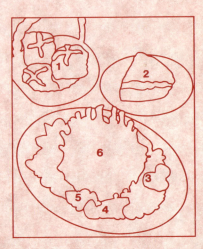

This is just the right size recipe to try if you're making this for the first time. Next time you will want to double it.

Warm water	½ cup	125 mL
Granulated sugar	1 tsp.	5 mL
Envelope active dry yeast	1	1
Butter or margarine, softened	¼ cup	50 mL
Granulated sugar	¼ cup	50 mL
Egg, room temperature	1	1
Salt	¾ tsp.	4 mL
Cinnamon	½ tsp.	2 mL
Warm milk	¾ cup	175 mL
All-purpose flour	1 cup	250 mL
Currants	½ cup	125 mL
Finely chopped, cut candied peel (optional)	2 tbsp.	30 mL
All-purpose flour	2¼ cups	550 mL

Stir water and sugar together to dissolve. Sprinkle yeast over water. Stir. Let stand 10 minutes. Stir.

Cream butter and sugar together. Beat in egg until fluffy. Mix in salt, cinnamon and milk. Beat in first amount of flour. Mix in yeast mixture.

Mix in currants and peel. Add remaining flour. Mix well, adding a bit more if necessary to make a soft dough. Let dough rest 10 minutes, then knead until smooth and elastic. Place in greased bowl turning to bring greased part to top of bowl. Cover. Let rise in a warm place to double in size, about 1 hour.

Punch dough down. Shape into about 18 balls. Place on greased baking sheet or 2 pans 8 × 8 inch (20 × 20 cm) allowing room for expansion. Cut a deep cross in each bun with lightly greased scissors or sharp knife. Cover and let rise until almost double in size or until light. Bake in 400°F (200°C) oven for about 20 minutes. Brush with butter and cool on rack. Ice crosses when cool. Makes about 18 buns.

GLAZE

Icing (confectioner's) sugar	½ cup	125 mL
Water	1½ tsp.	8 mL
Vanilla	¼ tsp.	1 mL

Mix all together adding a few more drops of water if needed to make a barely pourable glaze. Pipe or drizzle into crosses.

Pictured on page 53.

EASTER EGG BREAD

A braided loaf with colorful eggs nestled in among the braids. Eggs cook with the bread and are delicious.

Loaves of frozen bread dough	**2**	**2**
Raw eggs in shell, dyed pink, green blue, yellow	**6-8**	**6-8**

Thaw bread dough. Cut ⅓ from each loaf. Combine the 2 pieces to make 1 ball. Roll the 3 bread portions into long ropes about 24 inches (60 cm) long. Be sure to roll, not pull, to get the length. Pulling will tear bread. On large greased baking sheet lay the ends of the 3 ropes. Pinch the 3 ends together. Now braid the ropes. There is enough length to form a wreath shaped circle. Pinch second 3 ends to first 3 ends. Separate braids here and there and insert an egg in each hollow you make. Cover with waxed paper then a tea towel. Let rise until double in size. Remove covering. Bake in 375°F (190°C) oven for about 30 minutes. Brush with butter or margarine. Serves 8.

SHIRLEY TEMPLE/HE–MAN

A certain grandson, Jordon, won't drink this unless it is called He–Man.

Crushed ice	**½ cup**	**125 mL**
Pineapple juice	**2 oz.**	**60 mL**
Seven Up	**2 oz.**	**60 mL**
Grenadine syrup dash	**1**	**1**

Put crushed ice in glass. Pour in pineapple juice and Seven Up. Pour a dash of grenadine down inside edge of glass. Do not stir. Serve with a straw. Makes 1 drink.

*Everyone can tell at a glance that this delicate-yellow pie is home–
made. A real scene stealer.*

Water	**2 cups**	**500 mL**
Granulated sugar	**¾ cup**	**175 mL**
Lemon juice (fresh is best)	**½ cup**	**125 mL**
Butter or margarine	**1 tbsp.**	**15 mL**
Granulated sugar	**½ cup**	**125 mL**
Cornstarch	**6 tbsp.**	**100 mL**
Water	**¼ cup**	**50 mL**
Egg yolks	**3**	**3**
Salt	**¼ tsp.**	**1 mL**

**Baked pie shell, 9 or 10 inch (22 × 25
cm)**

Place first 4 ingredients in medium size saucepan. Heat over medium
heat until boiling. Stir often to dissolve sugar.

Combine remaining sugar and cornstarch in bowl. Stir thoroughly.
Add egg yolks and salt. Mix well. Pour slowly, while stirring, into
boiling water. Keep stirring until it boils and thickens. Continue to
simmer for 1 or 2 minutes to allow starchy taste to disappear. Remove
from heat. Let stand while making meringue.

MERINGUE

Egg whites, room temperature	**3**	**3**
Cream of tartar	**¼ tsp.**	**1 mL**
Granulated sugar	**6 tbsp.**	**100 mL**

Beat egg whites and cream of tartar in small mixing bowl (not plastic)
until stiff peaks form.

Add sugar gradually, while beating. No granules should be felt when
rubbing a bit of meringue between fingers. Pour lemon filling into
baked shell. Pile meringue on top. Push around edges to seal to crust.
Bake in 350°F (180°C) oven until golden brown, about 10 to 12 min–
utes. Cool at room temperature out of drafts for 2 to 3 hours at least
before cutting.

Pictured on page 53.

MOTHER'S DAY

To the sons and daughters of this world:

Mother's Day, as well as Father's Day, is a time for kids to get on the good side of Mom and Dad. Be sure you tell them "It's your day!".

How about pizza for breakfast? Does it sound like something only a kid would think of? Once Mom and Dad try the Breakfast Pizza, they will happily surrender the next time you ask. A container of Six Week Bran Muffin batter kept handy in the refrigerator will result in a freshly baked breakfast treat with little planning required. Drop the hint before that special day.

Flowers are a nice touch to adorn your parent's breakfast tray. Imagine the surprise when you walk through the door! Be careful not to trip!

Now for the real treat. After breakfast, be sure to clean up the kitchen.

MENU

Sunshine Frost
Fruit Medley

Breakfast Pizza
Currant Scones
Blueberry Muffins
Six Week Bran Muffins

Café Au Lait
Jiffy Hot Chocolate

SUNSHINE FROST

Fast and easy. No blender required.

Frozen concentrated orange juice	6 oz.	170 g
Frozen concentrated lemonade	6 oz.	170 g
Pineapple juice	48 oz.	1.4 L
Apricot nectar	12 oz.	341 mL
Seven Up or ginger ale	8 cups	2 L

Add all ingredients to punch bowl in order given. If not serving immediately save Seven Up until just before serving. Makes about 16 cups (3.6 L).

Pictured on page 71.

FRUIT MEDLEY

This is an opportunity to enjoy your favorite fruit in a simple or elaborate display.

Cantaloupe, peeled, seeded, cut bite size
Honeydew, peeled, seeded, cut bite size
Watermelon, peeled, seeded, cut bite size
Strawberries, left whole
Bananas, peeled, cut, dipped in orange juice
Kiwi fruit, peeled, sliced
Apples, unpeeled, cut in wedges, dipped in orange juice
Green grapes
Red grapes
Oranges, peeled, cut in wedges
Ripe pineapple, cut in chunks or spears
Papaya, peeled, seeded, cut bite size

Choose at least 3 or 4 different varieties keeping color in mind. Arrange in a pretty serving bowl or on a tray.

Pictured on page 71.

CURRANT SCONES

You will wonder how anything so good can be prepared so fast. Reprinted from Company's Coming Muffins & More.

All-purpose flour	2 cups	500 mL
Granulated sugar	¼ cup	50 mL
Baking powder	4 tsp.	20 mL
Salt	½ tsp.	2 mL
Cold butter or margarine	¼ cup	50 mL
Currants	½ cup	125 mL
Egg	1	1
Milk	⅔ cup	150 mL

Milk for brushing tops
Granulated sugar for sprinkling

In large bowl put flour, sugar, baking powder and salt. Add butter. Cut in until crumbly. Stir in currants. Make a well in center.

In small bowl, beat egg until frothy. Stir in milk. Pour into well. Stir with a fork to form soft dough. Turn out on lightly floured surface. Knead 8 to 10 times. Divide into two equal parts. Pat each into 6 inch (15 cm) circle. Transfer to greased baking sheet. Brush tops with milk and sprinkle with sugar. Score each top into 6 pie shaped markings. Bake in 425°F (220°C) oven for 15 minutes until risen and browned slightly. Serve hot with butter and jam. Yield: 12 scones.

Pictured on page 71.

BLUEBERRY MUFFINS

A good choice to serve with bran muffins or on their own.

All-purpose flour	2 cups	500 mL
Baking powder	2 tsp.	10 mL
Salt	½ tsp.	2 mL
Butter or margarine	½ cup	125 mL
Granulated sugar	1 cup	250 mL
Eggs	2	2
Milk	½ cup	125 mL
Vanilla	1 tsp.	5 mL
Blueberries, fresh or frozen	1 cup	250 mL

(continued on next page)

Mix flour, baking powder and salt in large bowl. Make a well in center.

In another bowl, cream butter and sugar. Beat in eggs 1 at a time. Add milk and vanilla. Mix. Pour into well. Stir just enough to moisten.

Fold in blueberries. Fill greased muffin cups ¾ full. Bake in 400°F (200°C) oven for 20 to 25 minutes until browned and an inserted toothpick comes out clean. Makes 1 dozen.

Pictured on page 71.

BREAKFAST PIZZA

Serve this egg and cheese pizza with or without toppings. A store–bought pizza crust speeds it up even more.

Tea biscuit mix	2¼ cups	550 mL
Milk	½ cup	125 mL
Butter or margarine	2 tbsp.	30 mL
Eggs	10	10
Water or milk	¼ cup	50 mL
Salt	1 tsp.	5 mL
Pepper	¼ tsp.	1 mL
Pizza or spaghetti sauce	½ cup	125 mL
Grated Mozzarella cheese	2 cups	500 mL
Bacon pieces (partly cooked), ham, hot or plain sausage (cooked) Sliced fresh mushrooms Sliced tomato		

Mix tea biscuit mix and milk together to make a soft dough. Pat onto greased 12 inch (30 cm) pizza pan. Bake in 375°F (190°C) oven for 15 minutes to partially cook.

Melt butter in frying pan. Add eggs, water, salt and pepper. Beat lightly with spoon to mix. Stir until cooked. Remove from heat.

Spread pizza sauce over crust in pan. Cover with scrambled eggs.

Sprinkle with grated cheese. Add any other toppings you prefer. Return to oven. Continue to bake for about 15 minutes or until topping is sizzling hot. Cuts into 8 pieces.

Pictured on page 71.

SIX WEEK BRAN MUFFINS

Bake muffins at a moment's notice. A homemade convenience food. Excellent!

All bran cereal	2 cups	500 mL
Boiling water	2 cups	500 mL
Salt	1 tsp.	5 mL
Cooking oil	1 cup	250 mL
Granulated sugar	2 cups	500 mL
Eggs	4	4
Buttermilk	4$\frac{1}{3}$ cups	1 L
All-purpose flour	5 cups	1.1 L
Natural bran	4 cups	1 L
Baking soda	3 tbsp.	50 mL
Raisins or currants	2 cups	500 mL

In extra large bowl or small plastic tub combine cereal, water and salt.

In mixing bowl cream cooking oil with sugar. Beat in eggs 1 at a time. Stir in buttermilk. Add to cereal mixture. Stir.

Add flour, bran, baking soda and raisins. Mix together. Store in covered container in refrigerator. Let stand overnight before using and use within 6 weeks.

To bake, fill greased muffin cups ¾ full. Bake in 400°F (200°C) oven for about 20 minutes. Let stand for 5 minutes then remove from pan. Makes 6 dozen.

Pictured on page 71.

CAFÉ AU LAIT

This is a pleasant change.

Strong hot coffee
Scalding hot milk
Granulated sugar (optional)

Proportions are equal amounts of coffee and milk. If possible, these are poured at the same time into cup. Sweeten if desired.

Pictured on page 71.

JIFFY HOT CHOCOLATE: Heat chocolate milk until scalding hot. Makes a delicious easy drink.

OUR NATION'S BIRTHDAY

Every nation has a birthday. It's a great day for a picnic. This can be a family picnic or a party where everyone helps out by bringing food.

There is nothing like the carefree feeling of packing a picnic basket off to a nice shady spot, spreading out a blanket and small tablecloth, then setting out the food. Appetites come running.

A check list is included so that important non-food items will be remembered. Don't forget that it is your country's birthday. If you are not able to watch fireworks, you can add your own sparklers or candles to a cake.

Picnic check list: Picnic basket for food, salt, pepper, sugar, cream, pickles, relish, ketchup, mustard, mayonnaise, horseradish and butter. A sturdy box for non-food items; blanket, small tablecloth, napkins, plates, serving spoons, carving and paring knives, forks, knives, teaspoons, cups, glasses, paper towels, dish cloth, small bowl for water, plastic pitcher, water jug, plastic bag for garbage and garden flowers complete with a container. Don't forget the bug repellant to keep the uninvited guests away!

Picnics are great outdoor excursions for kids of all ages.

MENU

Vegetable Terrine

Meat Loaf
Jellied Meat Loaf
Oven Fried Chicken

Pasta Salad
Baked Beans
Devilled Eggs

Lazy Daisy Cake
Strawberry Tarts
Lemonade

VEGETABLE TERRINE

Three colorful layers make up this different and impressive appetizer. Served cold, it is very tasty.

Eggs	2	2
Grated Cheddar cheese	½ cup	125 mL
Frozen broccoli, cooked, extra finely chopped (food processor works well)	10 oz.	284 g
Butter or margarine, softened	1 tbsp.	15 mL
Seasoned salt	¼ tsp.	1 mL
Eggs	2	2
Grated Cheddar cheese	½ cup	125 mL
Mashed cooked carrot	1 cup	250 mL
Butter or margarine, softened	1 tbsp.	15 mL
Seasoned salt	¼ tsp.	1 mL
Eggs	2	2
Grated Cheddar cheese	½ cup	125 mL
Cooked cauliflower, extra finely chopped	1 cup	250 mL
Butter or margarine, softened	1 tbsp.	15 mL
Seasoned salt	¼ tsp.	1 mL

In small bowl beat first 2 eggs with spoon. Add next 4 ingredients. Mix together well. Spread evenly in greased pan. Size 8 × 4 × 2⅜ inch (20 × 10 × 6 cm) is the best size to use.

In another bowl beat second 2 eggs with spoon. Add next 4 ingredients. Mix well. Spread evenly over broccoli mixture.

In third bowl beat remaining 2 eggs with spoon. Add next 4 ingredients. Mix together. Spread over carrot mixture. Smooth top. Bake in 325°F (160 °C) oven for about 1 hour, 15 minutes.

Cool, then chill well. To unmold, loosen edges with knife. Dip bottom into hot water. Unmold on plate. Cut into slices. Serve.

Pictured on page 89.

Made from scratch, these will bring back memories to many. No need to presoak beans but if you prefer to do so, you save about twenty minutes baking time. These may be completely cooked on top of the stove.

Navy beans	**2¼ cups**	**500 mL**
Water	**6 cups**	**1.4 L**
Molasses	**½ cup**	**125 mL**
Chopped onion	**½ cup**	**125 mL**
Brown sugar	**½ cup**	**125 mL**
White vinegar	**2 tbsp.**	**30 mL**
Bacon slices, cut up	**4**	**4**
Salt	**1 tsp.**	**5 mL**
Garlic powder	**⅛ tsp.**	**0.5 mL**
Ketchup	**¼ cup**	**50 mL**
Ketchup	**2 tbsp.**	**30 mL**
Bacon slices, cut up and half cooked	**2**	**2**

Place beans and water into large saucepan. Bring to a boil. Cover and simmer about 50 minutes until beans can be bitten into easily.

Add next 8 ingredients. Stir to mix. Transfer to bean pot. If there isn't room for all the liquid, save it to add as beans cook. Bake, covered, in 300°F (150°C) oven for 2½ hours.

Spread remaining ketchup over top. Put half cooked bacon over ketchup. Continue to bake, uncovered, for ½ hour or until cooked. Serves 8.

Note: To soak beans overnight, cover with lots of water. Drain next morning. Proceed as recipe states but simmer only about 35 minutes until beans can be bitten into easily.

Paré Pointer

Snakes make the worst mothers. They are so cold blooded.

JELLIED MEAT LOAF

This uses leftover roast beef or turkey.

Chopped cooked roast beef	3 cups	750 mL
Unflavored gelatin powders	3 x ¼ oz.	3 x 7 g
Cold water	¾ cup	175 mL
Chicken bouillon cubes	3 x ⅕ oz.	3 x 6 g
Boiling water	2¼ cups	500 mL
Salt	½ tsp.	2 mL
Onion powder	¼ tsp.	1 mL
Pepper	¼ tsp.	1 mL

Chop beef with knife into small pieces. If too large, loaf will not slice well.

Sprinkle gelatin over cold water. Let stand 5 minutes.

Dissolve bouillon cubes in boiling water. Add gelatin. Stir to dissolve.

Add salt, onion powder and pepper. Stir well. Add beef. Pour into 9 × 5 inch (22 × 12 cm) loaf pan. Chill, but be sure to stir occasionally while it is thickening. As soon as meat will remain suspended in gelatin, it will not require further stirring. Makes 1 loaf.

Picture on page 89.

SPEEDY BAKED BEANS

Easy to prepare and so delicious to eat. Rich color.

Bacon slices, diced	4	4
Finely chopped onion	1 cup	250 mL
Beans in tomato sauce or with pork	3 x 14 oz.	3 x 398 mL
Molasses	2 tbsp.	30 mL
Ketchup	¾ cup	175 mL
Brown sugar	¼ cup	60 mL

Sauté bacon and onion in frying pan until onion is soft and clear.

Mix bacon-onion mixture and remaining ingredients together in 1½ quart (1.5 L) casserole. Bake uncovered in 350°F (180°C) oven for about 1 hour. Serves 8 to 10.

The loaf of many uses. Serve hot from the oven or cut a thin cold slice for a sandwich or carry to a picnic. This loaf slices well when cold and holds together.

Bread slices	5	5
Cold water	¾ cup	175 mL
Lean ground beef	1¼ lbs.	565 g
Medium onion, finely chopped	1	1
Egg	1	1
Grated Cheddar cheese	¼ cup	60 mL
Salt	1 tsp.	5 mL
Pepper	¼ tsp.	1 mL
Tomato sauce	7½ oz.	213 mL

Leave crusts on bread. Break up into pieces in bowl. Add water. Let soak 2 or 3 minutes.

Add next 6 ingredients. Mix together well. Pack into 9 × 5 inch (22 × 12 cm) loaf pan.

Spread tomato sauce over top. Bake in 350°F (180°C) oven for about 1½ hours. Makes 1 loaf.

Pictured on page 89.

Paré Pointer

No wonder she looks so young for her age; it takes time to get old and she never had any.

POTATO SALAD

No picnic is complete without one.

Cooked potatoes, cubed	6 cups	1.4 L
Chopped green onions	4	4
Chopped celery	½ cup	125 mL
French dressing	¼ cup	50 mL
Mayonnaise	1 cup	250 mL
Sour cream	⅓ cup	75 mL
Salt	1 tsp.	5 mL
Pepper	¼ tsp.	1 mL
Hard-boiled eggs	4 - 6	4 - 6
Paprika		

Place potatoes, onion and celery in bowl.

Mix French dressing, mayonnaise, sour cream, salt and pepper together. Add to potato mixture. Toss to coat.

Chop eggs. Add and mix lightly. Transfer to serving bowl. Sprinkle with paprika. Serves 8 people, ¾ cup (175 mL) each.

Note: This has a slight cheesy color from the French dressing. Omit it if you want a whiter salad. Add a bit more mayonnaise. Sliced radish, cucumber, pickle, green pepper may be added.

DEVILLED EGGS

Always popular any time.

Hard-boiled eggs	8	8
Mayonnaise	⅓ cup	75 mL
Prepared mustard	½ tsp.	2 mL
Salt	¼ tsp.	1 mL
Pepper	⅛ tsp.	0.5 mL
Vinegar	1½ tsp.	7 mL
Paprika		

(continued on next page)

Cut eggs in half lengthwise. Remove yolks to bowl. Add remaining ingredients except paprika. Mash with fork until smooth. If too dry, add a bit of milk. Fill egg whites. Use a pastry tube for an artistic look. Arrange on plate.

Sprinkle with paprika. Serves 8.

Note: Hard-boiled eggs in the shell are suitable for a picnic also. Everyone gets to peel their own.

PASTA SALAD

Real tasty with bits of red and green showing through. Tangy.

Spaghetti twists	**4 cups**	**1 L**
Finely chopped green pepper	**2 tbsp.**	**30 mL**
Sweet pickle relish	**2 tbsp.**	**30 mL**
Chopped celery	**½ cup**	**125 mL**
Cheddar cheese, grated or diced	**½ cup**	**125 mL**
Chopped radish	**¼ cup**	**50 mL**
Onion powder	**¼ tsp.**	**1 mL**
Mayonnaise	**¾ cup**	**175 mL**
Salt	**1 tsp.**	**5 mL**
Pepper	**¼ tsp.**	**1 mL**

Cook spaghetti twists according to package directions. Rinse with cold water to cool. Drain very well.

Add remaining ingredients in order given. Mix together well. Chill until ready to serve. Makes about 4½ cups (1.1 L).

MACARONI SALAD: Use 2 cups (500 mL) elbow macaroni instead of spaghetti twists.

Pictured on page 89.

OVEN FRIED CHICKEN

This is oven-fried. Needs no attention. Excellent choice for picnics or any other time as well.

Chicken parts	**6½ lbs.**	**3 kg**
Dry fine bread crumbs	**2 cups**	**500 mL**
Salt	**2 tsp.**	**10 mL**
Pepper	**½ tsp.**	**2 mL**
Paprika	**2 tsp.**	**10 mL**
All-purpose flour	**1 cup**	**250 mL**
Milk	**1 cup**	**250 mL**

Melted butter or margarine

Have chicken parts mixed, dark and light meat. Cut chicken breasts in 4 pieces or 3 if breasts are small.

Mix crumbs, salt, pepper and paprika together.

Dredge chicken with flour. Dip in milk and coat with crumb mixture. Lay on baking pan skin side up. Bake in 350°F (180°C) oven for about 1 hour or until tender. Brush with melted butter immediately upon removal from oven. Serves 8.

Pictured on page 89.

MOTHER'S DAY

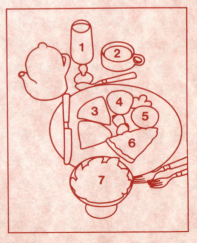

A white sponge-type cake that is iced, then caramelized in the oven.
Great flavor.

Eggs	2	2
Granulated sugar	1 cup	250 mL
Vanilla	1 tsp.	5 mL
All-purpose flour	1 cup	250 mL
Baking powder	1 tsp.	5 mL
Salt	¼ tsp.	1 mL
Milk, heated	½ cup	125 mL
Butter or margarine	1 tbsp.	15 mL

Beat eggs in mixing bowl until frothy. Beat in sugar in 4 or 5 separate additions. Stir in vanilla.

Stir in flour, baking powder and salt.

Heat milk and butter together in small saucepan until hot. Add, stirring carefully. Scrape into greased 9 × 9 inch (22 × 22 cm) pan. Bake in 350°F (180°C) oven until it tests done with toothpick, about 25 min–utes. Put on topping.

TOPPING		
Packed brown sugar	⅔ cup	150 mL
Butter or margarine	¼ cup	50 mL
Cream or milk	2 tbsp.	30 mL
Coconut	½ cup	125 mL

Combine all ingredients together in small saucepan. Heat and stir until hot and sugar is dissolved. Spread over cake. Return to oven until it bubbles well, about 3 to 5 minutes.

Variation: An equal amount of chopped nuts may be substituted for the coconut if preferred.

Pictured on page 89.

Paré Pointer

As the digital watch said, "Look, Ma, no hands".

STRAWBERRY TARTS

These fabulous tarts are a delight to the eye. Make lots.

Baked tart shells	12	12
Strawberries	4 cups	1 L
Water	1½ cups	350 mL
Granulated sugar	¾ cup	175 mL
Cornstarch	2 tbsp.	30 mL
Strawberry flavored gelatin	3 oz.	85 g

Have baked tart shells ready. Slice berries and fill. Small berries may be left whole.

Put water, sugar and cornstarch in small saucepan. Heat and stir until it boils and thickens. Remove from heat.

Add gelatin. Stir to dissolve. Cool. Put saucepan in cold water in sink to hasten cooling. Spoon over berries. Use a pastry brush for easy touch ups around edges that didn't cover when mixture was spooned over. Makes 12.

Note: This recipe will fill and glaze 2 dozen purchased, frozen 3 inch (7.5 cm) tart shells.

Pictured on page 89.

GRAPE PUNCH

A popular flavor.

Grape juice	4½ cups	1 L
Condensed frozen lemonade	6 oz.	170 g
Water	1 cup	250 mL
Ginger ale	6 cups	1.3 L

Combine grape juice, lemonade and water in punch bowl. Add a bit more ginger ale to taste if you prefer. Makes about 12 cups (2.7 L).

LEMONADE

The good old-fashioned kind complete with little bits of pulp. Syrup keeps for ages and also freezes.

Lemon rind	1 tbsp.	15 mL
Lemons	10	10
Granulated sugar	10 cups	2.25 L
Boiling water	10 cups	2.25 L
Citric acid	2 oz.	56 g
Tartaric acid	1 oz.	28 g
Epsom salts	1 oz.	28 g

Put grated lemon rind in large pot. Squeeze lemons. Add both juice and rinds to pot along with sugar. Pour boiling water over all. Measure in citric and tartaric acid and epsom salts. Stir to dissolve sugar. Let stand overnight. Strain. Put into containers.

To serve combine 1 part lemonade syrup to 4 parts water. Makes 17 cups (4 L) syrup.

Pictured on page 89.

CHOCOLATE CHIP COOKIES

Almost everybody's favorite. These are loaded with chips.

Butter or margarine	1 cup	250 mL
Granulated sugar	½ cup	125 mL
Brown sugar, packed	½ cup	125 mL
Eggs	2	2
Vanilla	2 tsp.	10 mL
All-purpose flour	2 cups	500 mL
Salt	1 tsp.	5 mL
Baking soda	1 tsp.	5 mL
Semisweet chocolate chips	2 cups	450 mL

Cream butter and both sugars together well. Beat in eggs 1 at a time. Mix in vanilla.

Add remaining ingredients. Mix well. Drop by small rounded spoon–fuls onto greased baking sheet leaving room for expansion. Bake in 375°F (190°C) oven for about 7 to 9 minutes. Makes 5 dozen.

LABOR DAY

Labor Day is a holiday for many, a day of satisfaction for jobs well done. So go ahead and reward yourself. Get away for the day or better yet have the whole gang over for a sizzling barbecue. Just light up the barbecue, sit back, relax and enjoy the warmth of the day. With the perfect combination of good company and delicious bar-becue favorites, you'll want to celebrate Labor Day everyday!

MENU

Harvest Punch
Cheese Ball
Minibobs

Barbecued Ribs
Barbecued Hamburgers
Dressy Dogs

Carefree Vegetables
Green Salad
Twenty Four Hour Coleslaw

Barbecue Breads

Peco Ice Cream
Yogurt Pound Cake

HARVEST PUNCH

A good thirst quencher.

Water	1 cup	250 mL
Granulated sugar	1 cup	250 mL
Frozen concentrated orange juice	12 oz.	341 mL
Frozen concentrated pink lemonade	12 oz.	341 mL
Water	9 cups	2 L
Lemon juice	1/4 cup	50 mL
Grenadine syrup	1/3 cup	75 mL
Ginger ale	7 cups	1.6 L
Orange and lemon slices		

Stir water and sugar in punch bowl until sugar dissolves.

Add next 5 ingredients. Chill until ready to serve.

Carefully add ginger ale. Float orange and lemon slices on top. Makes about 20 cups (4.5 L).

CHEESE BALL

Make this ahead of time. Freeze leftovers after reshaping into a ball.

Cream cheese, softened	2 x 8 oz.	2 x 250 g
Grated sharp Cheddar cheese	2 cups	500 mL
Finely chopped pimiento	1 tbsp.	15 mL
Finely chopped green pepper	1 tbsp.	15 mL
Finely chopped onion	1 tbsp.	15 mL
Worcestershire sauce	2 tsp.	10 mL
Lemon juice	1 tsp.	5 mL
Cayenne pepper	1/8 tsp.	0.5 mL
Salt	1/8 tsp.	0.5 mL
Chopped parsley or nuts		

Mix all ingredients except parsley and nuts. Shape into 1 or more balls or into logs.

Roll in parsley or nuts or a mixture of both. Freezes well. Serve with assorted crackers.

MINIBOBS

Make up an assortment. Place tray in easy reach for guests to help themselves.

Wooden skewers, fairly short
Prosciutto ham
Melon cubes or balls
Cheese cubes
Olives
Pineapple chunks
Salami cubes
Pickled onions

Thread at least 3 varieties or more on each skewer. Vary color of each as well as the combination. Makes a good fruit appetizer.

CAREFREE VEGETABLES

The only way to go. Vegetables cook in the oven all in one or two containers.

Large carrots	8 - 10	8 - 10
Large onions	5	5
Medium potatoes	8	8
Large parsnips	8 - 10	8 - 10
Water	1 cup	250 mL
Salt sprinkle		
Pepper sprinkle		
Dabs of butter		

Use large turkey size roaster. Cut carrots in half and place in roaster. Cut onions into wedges. Cut potatoes in half. Parsnips cook quicker so needn't be cut as small as carrots. Place all vegetables in roaster, grouping each kind together. Pour water into bottom. Sprinkle with salt and pepper. Drop dabs of butter here and there. Cover. Bake in 325°F (170°C) oven until tender, about 1½ hours. To serve, remove lid and place long handled spoon in roaster. Serves 8.

BARBECUED RIBS

These ribs are tender and cook quickly. The secret is in precooking.

Spareribs, cut in short lengths and 2 to 4 ribs in width	**6 lbs.**	**2.75 kg**
Water	**1 cup**	**250 mL**

Place ribs and water in roaster. Cover and bake in 350°F (180°C) oven for 1 hour or until barely tender. Cool a bit then chill in refrigerator until needed.

To cook on the barbecue, place ribs on tray along with Garlic Sauce. Arrange ribs over hot coals. When hot, turn and brush with sauce. Repeat on both sides. When sizzling and sauce is cooked in, remove from heat and serve. Serves 8.

GARLIC SAUCE

Brown sugar, packed	**1 cup**	**250 mL**
Cornstarch	**2 tbsp.**	**30 mL**
Garlic powder (or 2 cloves, minced)	**½ tsp.**	**2 mL**
Water	**1 cup**	**250 mL**
Soy sauce	**3 tbsp.**	**50 mL**

Mix all ingredients together in small saucepan. Heat and stir until it boils and thickens. Makes 1⅓ cups (300 mL) of good dark glaze.

Note: Tomato Sauce, below, is excellent on barbecued ribs also.

TOMATO SAUCE

An all round favorite. Zesty!

Condensed tomato soup	**10 oz.**	**284 mL**
Sweet pickle relish	**2 tbsp.**	**30 mL**
Dry onion flakes	**1 tbsp.**	**15 mL**
Brown sugar	**1 tbsp.**	**15 mL**
Worcestershire sauce	**1 tbsp.**	**15 mL**
Vinegar	**1 tbsp.**	**15 mL**

Combine all ingredients in saucepan. Heat and stir until boiling. Simmer 5 minutes. Great on barbecued ribs. Makes about 1½ cups (350 mL).

BARBECUED HAMBURGERS

People never tire of hamburgers.

Ground beef	3¼ lbs.	1.4 kg
Boiling water	½ cup	125 mL
Beef bouillon cube	1 x ⅕ oz.	1 x 6 g
Worcestershire sauce	1 tsp.	5 mL
Seasoned salt	½ tsp.	2 mL
Onion salt	½ tsp.	2 mL
Hamburger buns split, toasted and buttered	16	16

Mix meat with next 5 ingredients. Shape into 16 patties. Cook over hot coals for about 8 to 10 minutes on 1 side and about 5 to 7 minutes on second side. Sprinkle with salt and pepper after turning.

Insert patty in bun. Spread with Hamburger Sauce, below, or serve with condiments on the side such as ketchup, cheese, relish, lettuce, tomato, pickles, onion and mustard.

CHEESEBURGER: About 1 minute before hamburger patty is cooked, lay 1 cheese slice over top.

HIDDEN CHEESEBURGER: When shaping meat patties, make 2 thin patties instead of 1 thick. Put cheese between. Press edges to seal.

HAMBURGER SAUCE

Chili sauce	1 cup	250 mL
Ketchup	½ cup	125 mL
Prepared mustard	¼ cup	50 mL
Dry onion flakes or fresh onion (optional)	2 tbsp.	30 mL

Stir all ingredients together. Spoon over hamburger patty or directly on bun. Keeps for ages in refrigerator. Makes 1¾ cups (425 mL).

As for raindrops, two's company, three's a cloud.

TWENTY FOUR HOUR COLESLAW

Have on hand for any meal. Makes a good gift to take to a lake cottage.

Large cabbage, shredded	1	1
Large onion, finely chopped	1	1
Large green pepper, finely chopped	1	1
Medium carrot, shredded	1	1
Vinegar	2 cups	500 mL
Salad oil	1 cup	250 mL
Granulated sugar	3 cups	750 mL
Salt	4 tsp.	20 mL
Celery seed	4 tsp.	20 mL
Dry mustard powder	1 tsp.	5 mL
Pepper	½ tsp.	2 mL

Put cabbage, onion, green pepper and carrot into large bowl.

Measure remaining ingredients into large saucepan. Bring to boil, stirring frequently. Pour hot over cabbage mixture. Stir to mix, press–ing down until vegetables wilt and are covered with brine. Cool. Store in covered container in refrigerator. Let stand 1 or 2 days before eating.

very good
½ recipe good for 1 bag + coleslaw

DRESSY DOGS

A genuine frankfurter treat.

Wieners	16	16
Cheese slices	8	8
Bacon slices	16	16
Hot dog buns toasted and buttered	16	16

Cut wieners lengthwise almost to the bottom. Cut cheese slices in half. Insert ½ slice in wiener. Wrap diagonally with bacon. Secure with picks. Barbecue until bacon is cooked. Put into buns. Remove picks. Serves 8 allowing 2 hot dogs each.

HOT DOGS: Barbecue wieners until sizzling hot and browned a bit. Insert in bun. On the side serve cheese, onions, relish, mustard and ketchup.

GREEN SALAD

Dressing has a hint of dill which makes a nice change for a tossed salad.

GREEN DRESSING

Mayonnaise	½ cup	125 mL
Lemon juice	1 tbsp.	15 mL
Parsley flakes	1 tsp.	5 mL
Dried chives	½ tsp.	2 mL
Dried dill weed	⅛ tsp.	0.5 mL
Sugar	½ tsp.	2 mL

Mix all ingredients together. Let stand before using, preferably over–night.

SALAD

Mixed greens, spinach, Romaine, iceberg lettuce, amount equal to 1 head of lettuce		
Green onions, sliced	4	4
Cherry tomatoes, halved	16	16
Mushrooms, sliced	8 - 10	8 - 10

Combine in large bowl. Add dressing, thinning with milk if necessary. Toss lightly. Serves 8.

BARBECUE SAUCE

A dark red sauce with a mild smoky flavor. More smoky flavor can be added if desired.

Ketchup	2½ cups	625 mL
Corn syrup	½ cup	125 mL
Brown sugar, packed	½ cup	125 mL
Liquid smoke	2 tsp.	10 mL
Prepared mustard	2 tsp.	10 mL
Molasses	2 tbsp.	30 mL
Worcestershire sauce	1 tbsp.	15 mL

Heat all ingredients together in saucepan. Simmer for 2 to 3 minutes. Brush over steaks. Makes about 3½ cups (800 mL).

Prepare these well ahead. All are super good and are sure to be a hit at any feast.

Slice a French loaf in thick slices. If you are going to wrap in foil, cut slices all the way through. If you are going to heat loaf in oven unwrapped, cut slices almost to the bottom but not through it. Have butter or margarine at room temperature before beginning. Mix the ingredients of your favorite spread together and spread on both sides of cut slices. Reshape into loaf. Wrap in foil. Heat in 350°F (180°C) oven for 20 minutes, or heat on barbecue, turning often, for about 15 minutes. Wrap in 2 layers of foil to heat on barbecue. Or spread mixture on top of thick slices to broil in oven. Watch carefully as they burn easily. Before broiling, bread slices can be buttered then sprin-kled with flavoring ingredient. Saves time when time is at a premium.

CHEESE BREAD
Butter or margarine, softened	½ cup	125 mL
Grated Parmesan cheese	½ cup	125 mL
Soy sauce	1 tbsp.	15 mL

GARLIC BREAD
Butter or margarine, softened	½ cup	125 mL
Garlic salt or powder	½ tsp.	3 mL

GARLIC CHEESE BREAD
Cream cheese, softened	8 oz.	250 g
Milk	2 tbsp.	30 mL
Garlic salt	½ tsp.	2 mL
Horseradish	1 tbsp.	15 mL

HERB BREAD
Butter or margarine	½ cup	125 mL
Chives	2 tbsp.	30 mL
Garlic powder	¼ tsp.	1 mL
Parsley flakes	1 tsp.	5 mL
Thyme	½ tsp.	2 mL

OLD CHEESE BREAD
Butter or margarine, softened	½ cup	125 mL
Old Imperial cheese, softened	½ cup	125 mL

APPLE PIE

Serve warm or cold with cream, ice cream or cheese.

Pie crust pastry, your own or a mix

Cooking apples (such as MacIntosh), peeled, cored and cut up	5 cups	1.35 L
Granulated sugar	1 cup	250 mL
All-purpose flour	2 tbsp.	30 mL
Cinnamon (to taste)	¼ - ½ tsp.	1 - 2 mL

Granulated sugar for topping (optional)

Roll bottom pastry and fit into 9 inch (22 cm) pie pan. Cut off excess pastry.

Prepare apples. Set aside.

Mix sugar and flour together. Put about ½ into pie pan. Fill with apples. Sprinkle rest of sugar mixture over top. Sprinkle with cinnamon. Roll pastry. Dampen edges, cover with pastry. Cut off excess pastry. Press and crimp edges. Cut several slits in top. Sprinkle with a bit of granu–lated sugar. Bake in 350°F (180°C) oven until apples are tender, about 45 minutes.

Note: To use minute tapioca as a thickener instead of flour, sprinkle 1 tbsp. (15 mL) of tapioca over bottom crust followed by half the sugar, sliced apples, second half of sugar and cinnamon. Adjust sugar to ¼ cup (50 mL) less or more according to sweetness of apples.

PECO ICE CREAM

Try this lavish dessert to please young, old and in between. A great way to entertain young folks. Peanut butter is good for more than sandwiches.

Eggs	4	4
Granulated sugar	1¾ cups	325 mL
Whipping cream	4 cups	1 L
Milk	3 cups	750 mL
Chocolate syrup	2 cups	500 mL
Smooth peanut butter	1 cup	250 mL
Vanilla	1 tbsp.	15 mL
Salt	½ tsp.	2 mL

(continued on next page)

Beat eggs well. Add sugar and beat until light.

Add remaining ingredients. Beat to mix. Pour into 1 gallon (5 L) ice cream maker. Freeze according to freezer instructions. Makes 1 gallon (5 L).

Note: This may be made without an ice cream freezer. Combine sugar, milk, chocolate syrup, peanut butter, vanilla and salt in large heavy saucepan. Heat until simmering, stirring often. Beat eggs in small bowl. Stir some hot mixture into eggs then stir eggs into hot mixture. Cook, stirring often, for about 1 minute until slightly thickened. Pour into bowl. Chill. Beat cream until stiff. Fold into chilled mixture. Freeze. Makes a smooth and creamy ice cream.

PUMPKIN ICE CREAM

Turn out this positively brilliant ice cream to top off a meal or make it for an afternoon or evening snack.

Eggs	4	4
Granulated sugar	1¾ cups	325 mL
Brown sugar, packed	½ cup	125 mL
Canned pumpkin	4 cups	1 L
Whipping cream	4 cups	1 L
Milk	1 cup	250 mL
Vanilla	1 tsp.	5 mL
Cinnamon	1 tsp.	5 mL
Cloves	1 tsp.	5 mL
Ginger	1 tsp.	5 mL
Salt	½ tsp.	2 mL

In mixing bowl beat eggs. Beat in both sugars until light.

Add remaining ingredients. Mix together. Pour into 1 gallon (5 L) ice cream maker. Freeze as freezer manual directs. Makes 1 gallon (5 L).

Note: If you don't have an ice cream freezer, combine all ingredients except eggs and whipping cream in large heavy saucepan. Heat until simmering, stirring often. Beat eggs in small bowl until foamy. Stir some hot mixture into eggs then stir eggs into hot mixture. Continue to cook, stirring often, until thickened, about 1 minute. Chill thoroughly. Whip cream until stiff. Fold into chilled mixture. Freeze.

YOGURT POUND CAKE

You will love the texture of this tasty cake. Use as a coffeecake or dessert.

Egg whites, room temperature	6	6
Cream of tartar	¼ tsp.	1 mL
Granulated sugar	½ cup	125 mL
Butter or margarine, softened	1 cup	250 mL
Granulated sugar	1½ cups	375 mL
Egg yolks	6	6
Grated lemon rind	2 tsp.	10 mL
Lemon juice	2 tbsp.	30 mL
All-purpose flour	3 cups	750 mL
Baking soda	1 tsp.	5 mL
Salt	¼ tsp.	1 mL
Unflavored yogurt	1 cup	250 mL

Beat egg whites with cream of tartar until soft peaks form. Add first amount of sugar gradually, beating continually, until mixture is stiff and glossy. Set aside.

Cream butter and second amount of sugar. Beat in egg yolks 1 at a time. Mix in lemon rind and juice.

Add flour, baking soda and salt alternately with yogurt. Beat until smooth after each addition.

Gently fold egg whites into batter. Pour into a greased and floured 10 inch (25 cm) tube pan. Bake in 350°F (180°C) oven for about 1 hour. Cool. Remove from pan by loosening sides with knife. Invert on plate. Dust with icing (confectioner's) sugar before serving.

If five hundred Indians have no apples you could call them the Indian apple-less 500.

THANKSGIVING

A day set aside to celebrate the feast of the harvest. A time for gathering family and friends. A time to pause and give thanks both in church and at the dinner table for many blessings received.

Traditional Thanksgiving dinner boasts of plump golden turkey and pumpkin or pecan pie.

Decorate the table with colorful leaves of autumn, ripe grain stalks and an abundance of fruit. A cornucopia or horn of plenty is the most suitable of table centers symbolizing harmony, peace and plenty.

MENU

Roast Turkey
with
Gravy
Stuffing Simplified

Premium Potatoes
Acorn Squash
Zucchini Bake

Pink Cranberry Salad
Tossed Salad

Chow Chow

Pumpkin Pie
Pecan Pie

STUFFING SIMPLIFIED

Just the ticket for saving time. Streamlined to serve large quantities whether serving a few or a multitude. Flavorful and a snap to make.

Dry bread crumbs	5 cups	1.25 L
Dry onion flakes	¼ cup	60 mL
Parsley flakes	1 tbsp.	15 mL
Poultry seasoning	2 tsp.	10 mL
Salt	¾ tsp.	7 mL
Pepper	¼ tsp.	1 mL
Water (or more)	1¾ cups	425 mL

Mix first 6 ingredients together in large container.

Pour water over top. Toss to dampen evenly. Makes enough stuffing for a 10 to 12 lb. (4 kg to 5.4 kg) bird.

Note: To cook separately in a covered casserole or small roaster, lay thin slices of butter or margarine over top using at least ½ cup (125 mL). Pour some water around outside edge, about ¾ cup (175 mL). Bake in 350°F (180°C) oven for about 30 minutes until steaming hot. Halfway through cooking, stir and add more water if needed then or later.

Note: 1 cup (250 mL) chopped onion, sautéed first, may be used instead of instant.

Variation: Small dried bread cubes may be used for part of the bread crumbs.

OUR NATION'S BIRTHDAY

1. Lazy Daisy Cake page 73
2. Oven Fried Chicken page 70
3. Lemonade page 75
4. Pasta Salad page 69
5. Strawberry Tarts page 74
6. Jellied Meatloaf page 66
7. Meatloaf page 67
8. Vegetable Terrine page 64

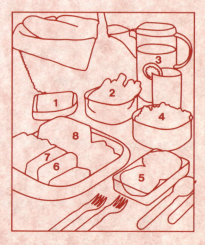

For Thanksgiving or Christmas or any big event, this is always a good choice.

Turkey	**12 lb.**	**5.5 kg**
Stuffing Simplified, see page 88	**12 cups**	**2.7 L**

Pack body cavity loosely with stuffing. Tie string around body and wings to hold wings close to body. Skewer skin together to hold stuffing inside. Tie legs to tail. Place on rack in roaster. Cover with lid or foil. If you prefer, leave uncovered in which case you will need to baste it a few times.

Roast in 400°F (200°C) oven for ½ hour to give it a good start but only if you have covered it. Reduce heat to 325°F (160°C) to finish cooking. If you prefer, oven may be at the lower temperature from the start. If using a meat thermometer inserted into thigh without touching bone, it should read 190°F (95°C) when done. If inserted from side of bird into center of stuffing it should read 165°F (75°C). Allow 5 hours to cook. If you don't have a thermometer, meat should show signs of coming off bone at end of leg. Drumstick meat should feel soft to press. Leg should move or twist easily when lifted. If breast is pierced, there should be no pink tinge to the juice. To brown, remove cover for last ½ hour.

Pictured on page 107.

GRAVY

Drippings from roaster	**¾ cup**	**175 mL**
All-purpose flour	**¾ cup**	**175 mL**
Salt	**¾ tsp.**	**3 mL**
Pepper	**¼ tsp.**	**1 mL**
Water (include drippings without fat)	**6 cups**	**1.35 L**

Remove turkey from roaster. Pour off drippings into container. Mea–sure amount required and pour into large saucepan. Add flour, salt and pepper. Pour half the water into roaster to blend with brown bits. Stir and pour into flour mixture along with other half of water. Heat and stir until it boils and thickens. Check for salt and pepper. It will probably need more. Makes 6 cups (1.35 L).

Note: If gravy is too pale, add a few drops gravy browner.

PREMIUM POTATOES

Prepare this whenever you have time. Just pop it in the oven later to heat.

Medium potatoes	10	10
Salted water		
Cottage cheese	1 cup	250 mL
Sour cream	1 cup	250 mL
Butter or margarine	½ cup	125 mL
Salt	1 tsp.	5 mL
Pepper	¼ tsp.	1 mL
Onion powder	¼ tsp.	1 mL

Cook potatoes in small amount of salted water. Drain. Mash.

Add cottage cheese and mash again. Add sour cream, butter, salt, pepper and onion powder. Mash well. Turn into 3 quart (3 L) cas–serole. Smooth top. Cover and bake in 325°F (160°C) oven for 30 minutes until piping hot. Serves 8.

ACORN SQUASH

Sweet and done up right.

Small squash	4	4
Butter or margarine	¼ cup	60 mL
Dark corn syrup or honey	¼ cup	60 mL
Salt	1 tsp.	1 mL
Pepper	¼ tsp.	1 mL

Cut squash in half. Remove seeds. Place cut side down on baking pan. Bake in 375°F (190°C) oven for 40 minutes.

Mix butter, honey, salt and pepper together. Turn squash cut side up. Divide syrup mixture among hollows, spreading around the inside. Continue to bake another 20 minutes or until cooked. Serves 8.

Pictured on page 107.

ZUCCHINI BAKE

This puffy vegetable dish goes with anything. Creamy color with lots of green bits showing. Very good.

Eggs	5	5
Cooking oil	$2/3$ cup	150 mL
Parsley flakes	1 tbsp.	15 mL
Salt	$3/4$ tsp.	4 mL
Pepper	$1/4$ tsp.	1 mL
Grated Parmesan cheese	$2/3$ cup	150 mL
Chopped onion	$1 1/4$ cups	300 mL
Grated zucchini	$3 3/4$ cups	900 mL
Tea biscuit mix	$1 1/4$ cups	300 mL

Beat eggs in mixing bowl until frothy. Mix in cooking oil, parsley, salt and pepper.

Stir in remaining ingredients in order given. Pour into shallow greased 9 inch (22 cm) casserole. Bake in 350°F (180°C) oven for about 35 minutes. Serve hot. Makes 8 servings.

Pictured on page 107.

CRANBERRY SAUCE

Its a snap to make your own. The end result is such a rich color.

Boiling water	1 cup	250 mL
Granulated sugar	1 cup	250 mL
Cranberries, fresh or frozen	2 cups	500 mL

Put water and sugar into saucepan. Boil together. Add cranberries. Cook until skins pop, about 5 minutes. Remove from heat. Sauce will thicken as it cools. Makes a generous 2 cups (500 mL).

Variation: Put cranberry sauce through a food mill. It makes a little less in quantity but is extra nice.

CHOW CHOW

An old-time pickle especially good with any meat and gravy. A family favorite. Makes a good gift. Reprinted from Company's Coming Cas–seroles.

Onions, sliced	5 lbs.	3.2 kg
Green tomatoes, very firm, sliced	16 lbs.	7.2 kg
Salt	1 cup	250 mL
Granulated sugar	5 lbs.	2.2 kg
Pickling spice in bag	3 oz.	85 g
Turmeric	2 tbsp.	30 mL
Vinegar	1½ - 2 qts.	1.5 - 2 L

Peel onions. Slice in ¼ inch (½ cm) slices. Cut up slices. Remove stem end from tomatoes. Slice in ¼ inch (½ cm) slices. Cut up slices. Slicing tomatoes after onions will remove onion smell from hands. Layer tomatoes, onions and salt in large, heavy preserving kettle. Cover. Let stand overnight.

Next day drain well. Add sugar. Secure pickling spice in bag made of any clean fabric — unbleached cotton is good. Push bag down among tomatoes. Add turmeric. Pour on vinegar until it reaches about 1 inch (2.5 cm) below surface of tomatoes. Too much vinegar will make too much juice. Bring to a boil, stirring frequently. Simmer about 2 hours. Remove spice bag and discard. Adjust sugar now. Go by taste. Add more if not sweet enough. Add more turmeric if needed to make a pleasing color. Pour into clean, sterilized jars. Seal. Yield: 9 to 10 quarts (9 to 10 L) or the equivalent in small jars.

Note: Do not use enamel container to make Chow Chow as it will scorch on the bottom.

Pictured on page 107.

Pare Pointer

The favorite dance of the Pilgrims was the Plymouth Rock.

PINK CRANBERRY SALAD

Add some color to the autumn decor of your table. Scrumptious.

Raspberry flavored gelatin	3 oz.	85 g
Pineapple juice from fruit plus water to make	1 cup	225 mL
Cream cheese	2 oz.	65 g
Crushed pineapple, drained	14 oz.	398 mL
Whole cranberry sauce	1 cup	250 mL
Whipping cream (or 1 env. topping)	1 cup	250 mL

Put gelatin and pineapple juice in saucepan. Heat and stir to dissolve. Add cheese in small pieces. Whisk well to blend in. Remove from heat.

Add pineapple and cranberry sauce. Chill until syrupy and thickened.

Whip cream until stiff. Fold into thickened mixture. Pour into mold. Makes about 5½ cups (1.25 L). Chill to set.

TOSSED SALAD

Simple and attractive.

Large bunch of greens, preferably mixed	1	1
Cherry tomatoes quartered	10	10
DRESSING		
Mayonnaise	½ cup	125 mL
Minced dill or sweet pickle	2 tbsp.	30 mL
Prepared mustard	1 tsp.	5 mL
Onion powder	¼ tsp.	1 mL
Granulated sugar	1 tsp.	5 mL
Milk	1 tbsp.	15 mL

Have greens and tomato ready in separate containers in refrigerator.

Dressing: Combine all ingredients together in small bowl. Mix well. Spoon over greens. Toss to coat. Add tomato and toss together lightly. Serves 8.

PUMPKIN PIE

Make for Thanksgiving or any time of year. Always a favorite.

Pastry for 2 pie shells

Eggs	4	4
Granulated sugar	1¼ cups	300 mL
Canned pumpkin	28 oz.	796 mL
Cinnamon	1½ tsp.	7 mL
Ginger	1 tsp.	5 mL
Nutmeg	½ tsp.	2 mL
Cloves	½ tsp.	2 mL
Salt	1 tsp.	5 mL
Milk (evaporated gives the best texture but part evaporated or all fresh milk may be used)	3 cups	700 mL
Whipping cream (or 2 env. topping)	2 cups	500 mL
Granulated sugar	2 tbsp.	30 mL
Vanilla	2 tsp.	10 mL

Line 2 pie pans, 9 inch (22 cm) size, with pastry.

Beat eggs in large mixing bowl until frothy. Beat in sugar. Add pumpkin, cinnamon, ginger, nutmeg, cloves and salt. Mix in.

Slowly mix in milk. Pour into pie shells. Bake on bottom shelf of 425°F (220°C) oven for 10 minutes. Turn heat down to 325°F (160°C). Continue to bake until a knife inserted near the centre comes out clean, about 1 hour. Cool.

Whip cream until stiff. Mix in sugar and vanilla. Spread over pies before serving. Makes 2 pies.

Note: Carrot Pie may be made using cooked mashed carrots in place of pumpkin. Every bit as delicious.

Pictured on page 107.

Be thankful for this incredible pie.

Butter or margarine	½ cup	125 mL
Granulated sugar	½ cup	125 mL
Eggs	3	3
Corn syrup	1 cup	250 mL
Vanilla	1 tsp.	5 mL
Pecans, halves or pieces	1 cup	250 mL
Unbaked pie shell, 10 inch (25 cm)	1	1

Cream butter and sugar together well. Beat in eggs, 1 at a time. Mix in syrup and vanilla.

Stir in nuts.

Pour into pastry shell. Bake on bottom shelf of 350°F (180°C) oven for about 45 minutes to 1 hour or until a knife inserted near center comes out clean.

POTATO SPOOF

The un-potato dish. Very good. May be prepared early in the day to heat when needed.

Long grain rice	1 cup	250 mL
Water	2 cups	500 mL
Salt	½ tsp.	2 mL
Grated Cheddar cheese	1 cup	250 mL
Sour cream	1 cup	250 mL

Put rice, water and salt in saucepan. Cook until tender.

Add cheese and sour cream. Bake uncovered in 350°F (160°C) oven for 30 minutes. Serves 4. Double recipe to serve 8.

HALLOWEEN

The night that goblins, witches and ghosts appear. But don't be afraid. It's all in the spirit of fun.

Halloween calls for an eerie setting of spiders, black cats, owls and bats. What seems like the occult is really just a fun time when scarey and ugly win out!

Easy-to-make decorations will set the scene. Have spiders, ghosts and scarecrows hanging from the ceiling. A jack-o'-lantern in the window will draw the demons to you! Blue and green Christmas lights will cast an eerie glow. Haunting music and witches' cackles will cause your guests to quiver.

Have prizes for those who bring the best carved pumpkin or whoever wears the most imaginative costume. Bring out the family skeleton. Bring on the tricks and treats!

MENU

Witches Brew
Saucy Meatballs
Bat Wings
Scarecrows On Sticks

Tiny Caldrons
Pumpkin Patch

Pink Popcorn Balls
Popcorn Balls
Candied & Caramel Apples

Halloween Cookies
Pumpkin Squares

WITCHES BREW

A spicy hot punch. Doubles easily. Good as it cools too.

Apple cider or juice	8 cups	2 L
Prepared orange juice	4 cups	1 L
Granulated sugar	2 cups	500 mL
Cinnamon sticks, 3 inch (7.5 cm) size	6	6
Whole cloves	12	12
Allspice powder	1/4 tsp.	1 mL
Ginger powder	1/4 tsp.	1 mL
Apples, oranges		

Measure all ingredients except apples and oranges in large pot. Bring to a boil. Boil 10 minutes. Strain. If using glass container, rinse with hot water to warm it before filling with hot punch. Float slices of apples and oranges on top. Makes about 11 cups (2.5 L).

Pictured on page 125.

BAT WINGS

These wings are the color of singed pumpkin with the nip of the fire that did the singeing.

Chicken wings	3 lbs.	1.25 kg
Spaghetti sauce	1 cup	250 mL
Cornstarch	1 tbsp.	15 mL
Granulated sugar	1 tsp.	5 mL
Seasoned salt	1/2 tsp.	2 mL
Cayenne pepper	1/4 tsp.	1 mL

Cut off wing tips and discard. Arrange on foil lined baking sheet with sides. Cook in 350°F (180°C) oven for 30 minutes.

Mix remaining ingredients together in small saucepan. Heat and stir until it boils and thickens. Brush wings with sauce. Return to oven for 10 minutes, brush again, cook 10 minutes more or until tender. Makes about 18 bat wings.

Pictured on page 125.

SCARECROWS ON STICKS

A really super finger food for a party. Pleases any age.

Wieners	6	6
Wooden picks	12 - 18	12 - 18
All-purpose flour	¼ cup	50 mL
Eggs	2	2
Club soda	¾ cup	175 mL
Cooking oil	2 tbsp.	30 mL
All-purpose flour	1 cup	250 mL
Salt	1 tsp.	5 mL
Pepper	¼ tsp.	1 mL

Dry fine bread crumbs
Fat for deep-frying

Cut wieners into 2 or 3 pieces each. Push sticks into cut end of each piece. Coat with flour. Set aside.

Beat eggs well. Add club soda, cooking oil, flour, salt and pepper. Beat until smooth.

Dip each piece into batter, roll in crumbs and drop gently, including pick, into hot fat 375°F (190°C) to cook until browned. Turn to brown both sides. Drain on paper towels. These may be put on a paper towel lined pan and kept warm in 300°F (150°C) oven until all are finished. Makes 12 to 18.

Pictured on page 125.

Paré Pointer

No wonder those scarecrows aren't any fun. They're a bunch of stuffed shirts.

This is one of those handy dishes that can be used as a main dish or as an hors d'oeuvre when entertaining. Tasty.

Ground beef	1 lb.	454 g
Dry bread crumbs	¼ cup	50 mL
Dry onion flakes	2 tbsp.	30 mL
Parsley flakes	1 tsp.	5 mL
Salt	1 tsp.	5 mL
Pepper	¼ tsp.	1 mL
Egg	1	1
Milk	¼ cup	50 mL
Butter or margarine	2 tbsp.	30 mL

Mix all together. Shape into 60 to 65 small balls the size of a walnut.

Melt butter in frying pan. Brown meatballs. May be chilled or frozen until ready to use. To cook, put meatballs into casserole and cover with Pineapple Sauce. Bake in 350°F (180°C) oven for about 40 minutes until hot.

Pictured on page 125.

PINEAPPLE SAUCE

Pineapple tidbits with juice	14 oz.	398 mL
Brown sugar, packed	1 cup	250 mL
Vinegar	½ cup	125 mL
Corn starch	2 tbsp.	30 mL
Soy sauce	1 tsp.	5 mL

Mix all together in saucepan. Heat and stir until it boils and thickens. Pour over meatballs.

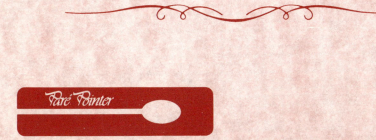

Pare Pointer

The fat ghost went on a diet so it could keep its ghoulish figure.

DEVIL'S DIP

Serve this special dip hot from the oven and watch it disappear. Just the right nip.

Cream cheese, softened	8 oz.	250 g
Sour cream	1 cup	250 mL
Jalepeño bean dip	10.5 oz.	298 g
Drops of tabasco	10	10
Dried chives	3 tbsp.	50 mL
Parsley flakes	2 tsp.	10 mL
Chili powder to cover	1 tsp.	5 mL
Grated Monterey Jack cheese	1½ cups	375 mL
Grated medium Cheddar cheese	1½ cups	375 mL
Chili powder sprinkle		

Mix first 6 ingredients together.

Spread in 9 x 13 inch (22 x 33 cm) pan.

Sprinkle first amount of chili powder over top, adding more if neces-sary to cover. Add layer of Monterey Jack cheese, then layer of Cheddar cheese. Sprinkle with chili powder. Bake in 350°F (180 °C) oven for about 20 minutes or as long as 40 minutes for a crispy effect.

Serve with Devil's Dippers, below, wheat thins, tortilla chips or other crackers. Makes 4 cups (500 mL).

Note: For a double devil's dip stir 2 tbsp. (30 mL) chili powder into the first 6 ingredients.

DEVIL'S DIPPERS

These can be an edible bouquet. Place in a glass tumbler beside the dip.

Carrots
Celery
Green onions

Devil's Fork: Slice carrot into wide thin slices. Cut into widest end about 2 inches (5 cm) making several narrow strips, forming fork tines.

Witches Broom: On end of celery stick, make as many cuts as possible about 2 inches (5 cm) long forming a broom.

Owls Roost: Slice ends of green onions to form a few branches.

No caldron ever held anything this good.

CREAM CHEESE PASTRY

Butter or margarine, softened	½ cup	125 mL
Cream cheese, softened	4 oz.	125 g
All-purpose flour	1 cup	250 mL

Beat butter and cream cheese until smooth. Work in flour. Roll into long thin roll. Mark off, then cut into 24 pieces. Press into tiny tart pans to form shells.

FILLING

Butter or margarine	1 tbsp.	15 mL
Finely chopped onion	1 cup	250 mL
Finely chopped mushrooms	1½ cups	375 mL
All-purpose flour	1 tbsp.	15 mL
Salt	½ tsp.	2 mL
Pepper	⅛ tsp.	0.5 mL
Thyme	⅛ tsp.	0.5 mL
Sour cream	⅓ cup	75 mL

Melt butter in frying pan. Add onion and mushrooms. Sauté until onion is clear and soft.

Stir in flour, salt, pepper and thyme. Mix in sour cream. Stir until thickened. Cool quite well. Divide among tart shells. Bake in 350°F (180°C) oven for about 20 minutes. Makes 24.

Pictured on page 125.

Paré Pointer

The first thing witches have to learn is not to fly off the handle.

PUMPKIN PATCH

Such nifty little things. Not as time consuming as they sound. Fun to make.

Cream cheese, softened	4 oz.	125 g
Grated sharp Cheddar cheese	1½ cups	300 mL
Worcestershire sauce	1 tsp.	5 mL
Onion powder	⅛ tsp.	0.5 mL
Garlic powder	⅛ tsp.	0.5 mL
Salt	⅛ tsp.	0.5 mL
Cayenne pepper	⅛ tsp.	0.5 mL
Rosemary sprigs	30	30

Measure first 7 ingredients into bowl. Mix together well. Shape into 30 small balls. Push on top to flatten each ball slightly. Indent tops with blunt object or your finger tip. Holding 1 in your hand, use dull side of knife to cut lines around ball.

Arrange on tray. Stick a piece of rosemary in each to form stem. Makes 30.

Note: To make these milder for a party for children use mild Cheddar cheese, omit cayenne pepper and add Worcestershire sauce to taste.

Pictured on page 125.

POPCORN BALLS

Fill a bowl with these tasty treats.

Popped popcorn	10 cups	2.25 L
Granulated sugar	1½ cups	350 mL
Water	½ cup	125 mL
Molasses	⅔ cup	150 mL
Vinegar	1 tsp.	5 mL
Salt	¼ tsp.	1 mL
Butter or margarine	3 tbsp.	50 mL

Have popcorn ready in large bowl. You will need to pop ½ cup (125 mL) of kernels. Do not salt.

(continued on next page)

Put sugar, water, molasses, vinegar and salt into heavy saucepan. Heat and stir until it begins to boil. Continue to cook without stirring to hard ball stage, 270°F (132°C), or until a bit dropped into ice water forms a hard ball that is pliable. Remove from heat.

Stir in butter. Pour over popcorn. Stir until all kernels are coated. With hands slightly buttered, form into 2½ inch (6 cm) balls using only enough pressure to shape. Makes about 15 balls.

Pictured on page 125.

CANDIED APPLES

These dazzling apples make quite a picture.

Firm red apples, medium size	8	8
Wooden sticks	8	8
Granulated sugar	3 cups	750 mL
Light corn syrup	½ cup	125 mL
Water	1 cup	250 mL
Cinnamon	¼ tsp.	1 mL
Red food coloring	¼ tsp.	1 mL

Wash, dry and polish apples. Remove stem. Insert wooden stick in stem end. Remove blossoms. Set aside.

Put sugar, syrup and water into saucepan. Heat and stir to dissolve. Boil without stirring until it reaches 300°F (150°C) on candy ther-mometer. A bit of syrup dropped into cold water will separate into brittle threads. Remove from heat.

Stir in cinnamon and food coloring. Dip apple to cover. Hold above saucepan to drain. Place on greased pan or tray stick side up. Quickly dip remaining apples. Return syrup to heat long enough to liquefy if it firms too much. Let stand at least 1 hour before serving. Makes about 8 apples.

Pictured on page 125.

CARAMEL APPLES

Make these from scratch. So good.

Firm apples, medium size	8 - 10	8 - 10
Wooden sticks	8 - 10	8 - 10
Evaporated milk	1⅓ cups	325 mL
Light corn syrup	½ cup	125 mL
Granulated sugar	2 cups	500 mL
Butter or margarine	1 tbsp.	15 mL
Vanilla	1 tsp.	5 mL

Wash, dry and polish apples. Remove stems and insert wooden sticks. Remove blossoms.

Put milk, syrup and sugar into heavy saucepan. Heat and stir to dissolve sugar. Boil, stirring continually, until thermometer reaches soft ball stage 240°F (115°C), or until a bit dropped into ice water forms a soft ball that will flatten easily. Remove from heat.

Stir in butter and vanilla. Dip apples to coat, holding over saucepan to drain. Place saucepan over heat to thin as needed. Place apples, stick side up, on greased pan or tray. Makes 8 to 10.

Pictured on page 125.

THANKSGIVING

1. Pumpkin Pie page 96
2. Acorn Squash page 92
3. Roast Turkey page 91
4. Chow Chow page 94
5. Zucchini Bake page 93

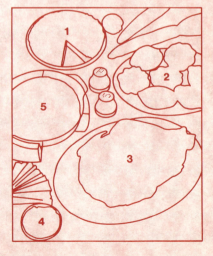

PUMPKIN SQUARES

These are very moist. It is almost like eating pumpkin pie out of your hand.

Butter or margarine	½ cup	125 mL
Granulated sugar	½ cup	125 mL
Brown sugar, packed	½ cup	125 mL
Eggs	2	2
Canned pumpkin	14 oz.	398 mL
All-purpose flour	1 cup	250 mL
Cinnamon	1 tsp.	5 mL
Nutmeg	¼ tsp.	1 mL
Ginger	¼ tsp.	1 mL
Baking powder	1 tsp.	5 mL
Baking soda	½ tsp.	2 mL
Salt	¼ tsp.	1 mL

Cream butter and sugar together. Beat in sugar then eggs 1 at a time. Slowly beat in pumpkin.

Add remaining ingredients. Stir. Scrape into greased 9 × 13 inch (22 × 33 cm) pan. Bake in 350°F (180°C) oven for about 25 minutes until an inserted toothpick comes out clean. Cool then frost with Cream Cheese Icing.

CREAM CHEESE ICING

Cream cheese, softened	4 oz.	125 g
Butter or margarine	¼ cup	50 mL
Vanilla	1 tsp.	5 mL
Icing (confectioner's) sugar	2 cups	500 mL

Beat cream cheese, butter and vanilla until smooth. Beat in icing sugar, a little at a time. Spread over Pumpkin Squares. Chill. Cuts into 54 moist squares.

Paré Pointer

It would be useless to hold a vampire race. They always finish neck and neck.

PINK POPCORN BALLS

Colorful and good.

Popped popcorn	**24 cups**	**5.5 L**
Salt (optional)		
Raspberry flavored gelatin (or any red gelatin)	**3 oz.**	**85 g**
Granulated sugar	**1 cup**	**250 mL**
Light corn syrup	**1 cup**	**250 mL**

You will need to pop a scant 1 cup (225 mL) of popcorn. Put in large bowl or pot and salt to taste.

Put gelatin, sugar and syrup into saucepan. Heat and stir to dissolve. Bring to a rolling boil. Pour over popcorn. Stir to coat well. Form into balls buttering hands as needed. Makes 24 balls, 2½ inch (6 cm) size.

Pictured on page 125.

CARAMEL WAFERS

A caramely treat that suits any sweet tooth. Try it with soda crackers too.

Graham crackers		
Butter or margarine	**1 cup**	**250 mL**
Brown sugar, packed	**¾ cup**	**175 mL**
Flaked almonds	**½ cup**	**125 mL**

Line greased 10 × 15 inch (25 × 38 cm) pan with crackers.

Put butter and sugar into saucepan. Bring to boil stirring occasionally. Boil 3 minutes. Spoon evenly over crackers in pan.

Sprinkle almonds over top. Bake in 350°F (180°C) oven for 7 minutes. Cuts into 20 pieces.

Note: Chopped walnuts make a good substitute for almonds. More economical as well. Ground pecans are superb.

Frosted or not, these add to the fun.

Butter or margarine	1 cup	250 mL
Granulated sugar	1½ cups	375 mL
Eggs	2	2
Vanilla	1 tsp.	5 mL
All-purpose flour	3 cups	750 mL
Baking powder	2 tsp.	10 mL
Salt	¼ tsp.	1 mL

Cream butter and sugar together well. Beat in eggs 1 at a time. Add vanilla.

Mix in flour, baking powder and salt. Roll out thickness of pie crust on lightly floured surface. Cut into 3 inch (7.5 cm) rounds. Bake in 350°F (180°C) oven for 8 to 10 minutes. Makes about 5 dozen.

HALLOWEEN COOKIES: Cut into shape of pumpkin, skeleton, ghost, owl or your favorite goblin. Leave plain or decorate with icing.

ICING		
Icing (confectioner's) sugar	1½ cups	350 mL
Butter or margarine	3 tbsp.	50 mL
Vanilla	½ tsp.	2 mL
Water or milk	5 tsp.	25 mL
Food coloring		

Beat all 4 ingredients together in bowl adding more icing sugar or water to make proper consistency. Tint desired color and pipe designs on cookies.

Pictured on page 125.

Pare Pointer

The little skeleton didn't want to go to school. His heart wasn't in it.

CHRISTMAS

A holy day steeped in tradition. Christmas spirit is the feeling of total well being, of smiles and season's greetings. It is a time of good will and good cheer, of giving and receiving, of families and friends reuniting and of brightly decorated surroundings. It is a time to share with children the story of the first Christmas.

Every family has a traditional Christmas meal. Although many asso-ciate turkey with Christmas, goose is a popular alternative. It is possible to vary your menu without breaking tradition.

MENU

Egg Nog

Shrimp Cocktail

**Roast Goose
with
Gravy
Fruit Stuffing**

**Potatoes Extraordinaire
Special Turnip
Frenched Beans**

Cranberry Orange Salad

**Chow Chow
Apple Sauce**

**Christmas Pudding
Rum Sauce
Mince Pie**

This is a light fluffy egg nog. The best. It can be left plain, without adding liquor, if desired.

Eggs	**12**	**12**
Icing (confectioner's) sugar	**3¼ cups**	**750 mL**
Salt	**½ tsp.**	**2 mL**
Vanilla	**¼ cup**	**50 mL**
Milk	**10 cups**	**2.25 L**
Brandy (or rum, rye, scotch)		
Nutmeg for garnish		

Using a large mixing bowl, beat eggs until very light and lemon colored.

Gradually beat in sugar, salt and vanilla. Stir in milk, using larger container if necessary. Add liquor. Refrigerate for 24 hours before serving. To serve, run through blender to foam up. To store for a few days, keep covered in refrigerator. Strength may be adjusted by adding more or less liquor or more or less milk. Garnish with nutmeg. Yield: 25 servings, 5 oz. (140 mL) each.

SHRIMP COCKTAIL

A family favorite to begin a favorite family meal. Reprinted from Company's Coming Appetizers.

Crisp lettuce, shredded	**1½ cups**	**375 mL**
Medium shrimp, rinsed and drained	**4 oz.**	**113 g**
Chili sauce	**¾ cup**	**150 mL**
Lemon juice	**2 tsp.**	**10 mL**
Worcestershire sauce	**¼ - 1 tsp.**	**1 - 5 mL**
Onion powder	**½ tsp.**	**2 mL**
Salt	**¼ tsp.**	**1 mL**
Peeled and diced apple	**½ cup**	**125 mL**
Finely chopped celery	**¼ cup**	**50 mL**

Line sherbet glasses with lettuce. Divide shrimp among sherbets, saving a few for garnish if desired.

Mix remaining ingredients in bowl, using smallest amount of Worces—tershire sauce. Add until the right amount for you is reached. Spoon over shrimp shortly before serving. Serve with 2 small mild flavored crackers placed beside each cocktail. Makes 4 to 5 servings.

ROAST GOOSE

Well suited to the holiday season, the Christmas goose has now been replaced by turkey in many homes.

Goose	**12 lbs.**	**5.5 kg**
Fruit Stuffing		

Stuff goose and fasten skin together with skewer. Tie legs to tail and wings close to body. Prick skin here and there to allow fat to run out. Roast in uncovered roaster (or cover if you prefer) in 450ºF (230ºC) oven for 30 minutes then at 350ºF (180ºC) until meat thermometer reaches 190ºF (87ºC), 3½ to 4 hours. Serves 12.

FRUIT STUFFING

Bread, day old, crusts removed and cut into cubes	**8 cups**	**2 L**
Chopped apples, unpeeled	**2 cups**	**500 mL**
Coarsely chopped dried apricots	**1 cup**	**250 mL**
Chopped onion	**1 cup**	**250 mL**
Raisins	**1½ cups**	**375 mL**
Poultry seasoning	**2 tsp.**	**10 mL**
Salt	**2 tsp.**	**10 mL**
Pepper	**¼ tsp.**	**1 mL**

Measure all ingredients into bowl. Mix well to distribute spices. Stuff goose.

GRAVY

Drippings from goose	**¾ cup**	**175 mL**
All-purpose flour	**¾ cup**	**175 mL**
Salt	**1 tsp.**	**5 mL**
Pepper	**¼ tsp.**	**1 mL**
Water (include drippings without fat)	**6 cups**	**1.5 L**

Remove goose from roaster. Pour all liquid from pan. Put measured drippings back into roaster. Mix drippings, flour, salt and pepper together. Stir in water until it boils and thickens. If too pale, add a bit of gravy browner. Check for salt. It may need more. Makes 6 cups (1.5 L).

Pictured on page 143.

POTATOES EXTRAORDINAIRE

A wonderful make ahead that tastes fresh with all the trimmings. Can be made in the morning to be heated later in the day or can be prepared a day or more in advance. May be halved for fewer appe–tites. Can be frozen.

Potatoes	**5 lbs.**	**2.27 kg**
Cream cheese, softened	**8 oz.**	**250 g**
Sour cream	**1 cup**	**250 mL**
Butter or margarine	**¼ cup**	**50 mL**
Onion salt	**1 tbsp.**	**15 mL**
Salt	**1 tsp.**	**5 mL**
Pepper	**¼ tsp.**	**1 mL**

Butter and paprika for garnish

Cook potatoes as usual in salted water until tender. Drain. Mash well.

Add cream cheese in pieces. Add next 5 ingredients. Beat until smooth and fluffy. Scrape into 2 quart (2 L) casserole.

Place dabs of butter here and there over top of potatoes. Sprinkle with paprika. Cover and heat in 350°F (180°C) oven until heated through. Makes about 12 servings.

FRENCHED BEANS

Prepare early in the day. Creamy and nutty. May be baked in the oven or heated in a saucepan.

Frozen frenched green beans, cooked	**6 cups**	**1.35 L**
Condensed cream of mushroom soup	**10 oz.**	**284 mL**
Sliced mushrooms, drained	**10 oz.**	**284 mL**
Flaked or slivered almonds, toasted in 350°F (180°C) oven 5 to 7 minutes	**¼ cup**	**50 mL**

Mix beans, soup and mushrooms together gently. Add about ¾ of the almonds saving the rest to sprinkle on top. Put bean mixture into casserole. Sprinkle with remaining almonds. Bake uncovered in 350°F (180°C) oven for 20 to 30 minutes until bubbly hot. Serves 8.

Note: Canned frenched beans may be used. Drain 3 cans, 14 oz. (398 mL) size and use instead of frozen.

Pictured on page 143.

SPECIAL TURNIP

Layered with sugared apples, this makes a nice color contrast.

Mashed turnip	4 cups	1 L
Butter or margarine	1 tbsp.	15 mL
Thinly sliced cooking apple, peeled	1½ cups	375 mL
Brown sugar, packed	¼ cup	60 mL
Pinch of cinnamon		
All-purpose flour	⅓ cup	75 mL
Brown sugar, lightly packed	⅓ cup	75 mL
Butter or margarine	2 tbsp.	30 mL

Mix turnip with butter to distribute.

In small bowl, toss apple, first amount of brown sugar and cinnamon together. Put layers of this with turnip in casserole beginning and ending with turnip.

Crumble flour, second amount of brown sugar and butter together. Sprinkle over top. Bake uncovered in 350°F (180°C) oven for 1 hour. Serves 8.

CRANBERRY ORANGE SALAD

A dark colored mold with a good flavor. Complete with orange, apple and nuts.

Lemon flavored gelatin	3 oz.	85 g
Boiling water	1 cup	225 mL
Cold water	½ cup	125 mL
Medium apple, peeled and grated	1	1
Canned whole cranberry sauce	1 cup	250 mL
Canned mandarin oranges, drained and cut into thirds	10 oz.	284 mL
Chopped pecans or walnuts	⅓ cup	75 mL

In medium bowl dissolve gelatin in boiling water. Add cold water. Chill until consistency of syrup. Stir occasionally.

Add remaining ingredients. Stir to distribute well. Pour into mold. Chill. Serves 8 to 12.

Pictured on page 143.

GREEN GODDESS SALAD

Just a great addition to any meal. Makes a large salad. To cut in size, use only part of dressing on quantity of lettuce required.

Head lettuce, medium	2	2
Mayonnaise	1 cup	250 mL
Sour cream	½ cup	125 mL
Chopped green onion	¼ cup	50 mL
Chopped parsley	¼ cup	50 mL
Anchovy paste	2 tsp.	10 mL
Worcestershire sauce	1 tsp.	5 mL
Prepared mustard	½ tsp.	2 mL
Salt	½ tsp.	2 mL
Pepper	⅛ tsp.	0.5 mL
Garlic powder (or 1 clove, minced)	¼ tsp.	1 mL
Cooked crab or shrimp	1 cup	250 mL

Have lettuce in bite size pieces in refrigerator.

Combine remaining ingredients except seafood in bowl. Beat with spoon to blend. Makes 2 cups (500 mL) dressing.

To serve, put lettuce, dressing and crab into large bowl. Toss well. Serves 12 to 15.

APPLE SAUCE

Home made is definitely the best. Use hot or cold.

Cooking apples such as MacIntosh	4	4
Water	½ cup	125 mL
Granulated sugar	¼ cup	60 mL
Cinnamon (optional)		

Peel and core apples. Cut into pieces. Put into saucepan. Add water. Bring to a boil. Cover and simmer gently until tender. Stir occasion–ally.

Mix in sugar. Remove from heat. Taste. Add more sugar if needed and add a bit more water if you want a thinner sauce. For a cinnamon flavor, stir in a small amount to taste while sauce is hot. Makes about 2 cups (500 mL).

TOURTIÈRE

Traditionally served in French Canadian homes Christmas eve.

Lean ground beef	2 lbs.	900 g
Ground pork	2 lbs.	900 g
Medium onion, chopped	1	1
Water	4½ cups	1 L
Medium potatoes, peeled and diced	3	3
Pickling spice, tied in cotton bag or disposable dish cloth	3 tbsp.	50 mL
Salt	1½ tsp.	7 mL
Pepper	½ tsp.	2 mL
Garlic powder	¼ tsp.	1 mL
Pie crust pastry		

Combine ground beef, pork, onion and water in large pot. Heat to boiling, stirring often. Boil slowly for 15 minutes.

Add potatoes and pickling spice. Simmer, covered, for 1 hour. Push spice bag down occasionally.

Add salt, pepper and garlic powder. Continue to simmer for ½ hour. Mash potatoes in pot as well as possible. Cool to lukewarm.

Roll out pastry to fit pans. Fill with meat filling. Dampen edge, cover with rolled pastry and crimp edges to seal. Cut slits in top. Bake in 400°F (200°C) oven for about 30 minutes or until browned. Makes 10 pies, 4 inches (10 cm) each or 6 pies, 5 inches (13 cm) each or 5 pies, 7 inches (18 cm) each.

If you combine a goose and a rhinoceros you would at least hear a honk before it ran you down.

CHRISTMAS PUDDING

Makes a dark and moist carrot pudding. Rum sauce and ice cream make it complete.

Ground beef suet	1 cup	250 mL
Brown sugar, packed	1 cup	250 mL
Grated potato	1 cup	250 mL
Grated carrot	1 cup	250 mL
Grated peeled apple	1 cup	250 mL
Raisins	1 cup	250 mL
Currants	1 cup	250 mL
All-purpose flour	2 cups	500 mL
Baking soda	1 tsp.	5 mL
Salt	1 tsp.	5 mL
Cinnamon	1 tsp.	5 mL
Allspice	½ tsp.	2 mL
Chopped walnuts (optional)	1 cup	250 mL

Mix all together in order given. Spoon into greased 10 cup (2.5 L) pudding pan. Cover with foil, tying sides down with string. Put in steamer with boiling water half way up sides of pudding. Steam for 3 to 4 hours adding more boiling water as needed. Serve with Rum Sauce, below. Serves 12 to 15.

RUM SAUCE

Put a cap on the pudding.

Brown sugar, packed	1 cup	250 mL
All-purpose flour	¼ cup	60 mL
Salt	½ tsp.	2 mL
Water	2 cups	500 mL
Vanilla	1 tsp.	5 mL
Rum flavoring	1 tsp.	5 mL

Mix sugar, flour and salt together in medium size saucepan. Stir well.

Add water and flavorings. Heat and stir until it boils and thickens. Serve over steamed puddings. Makes 2½ cups (625 mL).

BROWN SUGAR SAUCE: Omit rum flavoring. Dark brown sugar is best with this and with Rum Sauce.

MINCE TARTS

These have a milder mincemeat flavor than the usual. Keeps for ages in the freezer. Recipe may be halved or quartered. They come with lids on them. Reprinted from Company's Coming Desserts.

Pie pastry, your own or a mix

Mincemeat	**4 cups**	**1 L**
Canned apple sauce	**14 oz.**	**398 mL**
Minute tapioca	**3 tbsp.**	**50 mL**

Roll out pastry. Cut in circles to fit muffin cups. Cut smaller circles to fit top.

Stir mincemeat, (excellent if put in blender first), apple sauce and tapioca together. Fill shells. Moisten edges. Press top pastry circles around edges to seal. Cut 2 or 3 small slits in top. Sprinkle with a bit of granulated sugar. Bake on lowest shelf in 400°F (200°C) oven until browned. Serve warm with ice cream. They freeze well.

Note: Tiny tarts may be made to add to an assortment of holiday goodies. Lids may be omitted or small circles of pie crust can be baked separately to top each tart later.

MINCE PIE: Roll pastry to fit 9 inch (22 cm) pie pan. Fill pastry shell with a mixture of 2¼ cups (500 mL) mincemeat and 1 cup (250 mL) thick apple sauce. If apple sauce is thin stir in 1½ tbsp. (25 mL) minute tapioca. Dampen edges. Cover with pastry. Press edges to seal and flute. Cut slits in top. Sprinkle with a little granulated sugar. Bake on bottom shelf in 400°F (200°C) oven until browned, about 30 minutes. Serve hot. May be reheated in 325°F (160°C) oven for about 20 to 30 minutes. Cuts into 6 or 7 pieces.

Paré Pointer

A tree has it both ways. First it's chopped down, then it's chopped up.

NEW YEAR'S EVE

For many, New Year's Eve means gala parties, balloons, noise makers, party hats and streamers. For others, it means a quiet intimate evening with family and friends. For all of us it is a time to reminisce the good time had in the year gone by and to make grand resolutions for the new year about to begin.

Fonduing is conducive to conversation and relaxation. At the end of the festive season try it for a delightful change.

MENU

Appetizer Fondue
Fondue Pot

Teriyaki Sauce
Curry Sauce
Sweet And Sour Sauce

Battered Vegetables

Caesar Salad

Chocolate Fondue Sauce
Dessert Fondue Dippers
Father Time Cake

APPETIZER FONDUE

This serves as an appetizer or first course. So easy to assemble. Keep heat very low to avoid cheese going stringy.

CHEESE FONDUE SAUCE

Condensed Cheddar cheese soup	**10 oz.**	**284 mL**
Grated Farmers or mild Cheddar cheese	**1 cup**	**250 mL**
Grated Parmesan cheese	**4 oz.**	**125 g**
Green onions, finely chopped	**2**	**2**
Garlic powder	**⅛ tsp.**	**0.5 mL**
Dash of tabasco		

Measure all ingredients into heavy saucepan. Heat and stir over low heat until melted and hot. Transfer to fondue pot. If sauce gets too thick, dilute with white wine, beer or fruit juice. Use any or all of the following dippers.

DIPPERS
French bread cut in 1 inch (2.5 cm)
   cubes
Apple slices dipped in lemon juice
Seedless grapes, stems removed
Pimiento stuffed olives

Arrange food around fondue pot or in a separate bowl along with a fondue fork for each person to spear a piece of food and dip it in the hot cheese sauce. Serve white wine or ginger ale to complete a fun and different first course.

Paré Pointer

He got his flat tire from a fork in the road.

FONDUE POT

Gather around the table with your friends to cook your entrée to perfection.

Steak: Cut filet or sirloin steak into small cubes.

Chicken: Cut boneless chicken breasts into bite size pieces.

Ham: Cut ham into cubes.

Scallops: Cut large scallops in half.

Shrimp: Use bite size or cut large shrimp.

Fill fondue pot half full with cooking oil. Heat on stove burner first then put in center of table over heat.

Have meat at room temperature before frying. Blot with paper towels if there is excess moisture. Spatters are reduced if you add 1 tsp. (5 mL) salt to oil.

Serve a fondue fork for spearing and cooking and a dinner fork to eat with. The fondue fork will be much too hot.

Have individual dishes for sauces and for dippers. Place bowls of extra dippers on table.

TERIYAKI SAUCE

This makes a dark sauce. A touch of the Orient.

Beef bouillon cubes	2 x 1/5 oz.	2 x 6 g
Boiling water	2 cups	450 mL
Soy sauce	1/3 cup	75 mL
Granulated sugar	1/4 cup	50 mL
Garlic powder	1/4 tsp.	1 mL
Ginger	1/2 tsp.	2 mL
All-purpose flour	2 tbsp.	30 mL

Dissolve bouillon cubes in boiling water in saucepan. Add soy sauce.

Mix next 4 ingredients together well. Stir into bouillon mixture. Heat and stir until it boils and thickens. Makes about 2 cups (450 mL).

SWEET AND SOUR SAUCE

Dark and delicious.

Brown sugar, packed	2 cups	500 mL
All-purpose flour	2 tsp.	10 mL
Vinegar	½ cup	125 mL
Water	⅓ cup	75 mL
Soy sauce	2 tbsp.	30 mL
Ketchup	2 tbsp.	30 mL

In small saucepan thoroughly mix sugar and flour. Stir in vinegar, water, soy sauce and ketchup. Heat and stir over medium heat until it boils and thickens. Makes ¾ cup (175 mL).

CURRY SAUCE

Smooth.

Mayonnaise	1 cup	250 mL
Curry powder (start with less)	1 tbsp.	15 mL
Lemon juice	½ tsp.	2 mL
Paprika	½ tsp.	2 mL
Onion powder	⅛ tsp.	0.5 mL

Mix all together. Makes 1 cup (250 mL).

HALLOWEEN

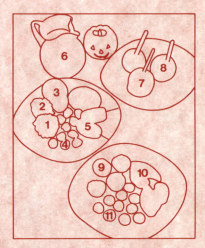

DILL SAUCE

A good dipping sauce, especially for meatballs.

Butter or margarine	**2 tbsp.**	**30 mL**
All-purpose flour	**2 tbsp.**	**30 mL**
Water	**1 cup**	**250 mL**
Sour cream	**½ cup**	**125 mL**
Ketchup	**1 tbsp.**	**15 mL**
Dry dillweed	**1 tsp.**	**5 mL**

Melt butter in small saucepan. Mix in flour. Add water. Stir or whisk until it boils and thickens.

Add sour cream, ketchup and dill. Stir to mix. Makes about 1½ cups (375 mL).

SWEET MUSTARD SAUCE

Mild and sweet.

Brown sugar, packed	**¾ cup**	**175 mL**
All-purpose flour	**2 tbsp.**	**30 mL**
Prepared mustard	**2 tbsp.**	**30 mL**
Salt	**¼ tsp.**	**1 mL**
Water	**1½ cups**	**350 mL**

Put sugar and flour into small saucepan. Mix together well. Add mustard, salt and water. Heat and stir over medium heat until it boils and thickens. Makes about 1 cup (250 mL).

Carry Me Back to Old Virginny was actually written by a lazy South–erner.

BATTERED VEGETABLES

Prepare vegetables beforehand. Set out ready to be dipped in batter then deep fried.

Broccoli: Cut bite size. Cook until barely tender. Drain.

Cauliflower: Cut bite size. Cook until barely tender. Drain.

Mushrooms: Use small whole mushrooms. Do not cook.

Onion Rings: Slice onions. Separate into rings. May be soaked in cold water ½ to 1 hour. Drain. Pat dry. Do not cook.

Parsnips: Cut bite size. Cook until barely tender. Drain.

Zucchini: Do not peel. Cut into short strips. Do not cook.

VEGETABLE BATTER

Pancake mix	1½ cups	375 mL
Club soda	1½ cups	375 mL

Beat together well with spoon. Add more club soda if too thick. Chill until needed. Have vegetables on individual plates or in larger bowls. Serve with a fondue fork to spear vegetable, dip in batter and cook in oil. Also give everyone a dinner fork to eat cooked morsels with as the fondue fork will be too hot.

TOMATO BEAN SALAD

A colorful dish to brighten any table.

Cut green beans, drained	14 oz.	398 mL
Ripe tomatoes, cut bite size	2	2
Italian dressing	3 tbsp.	50 mL

Combine all 3 ingredients in bowl. Stir. Turn into serving bowl. Makes 4 cups (1 L).

CHOCOLATE FONDUE SAUCE

Only three ingredients in this smooth as satin topping. Serve hot or cold. Also makes a good fondue dip.

Evaporated milk	1 cup	250 mL
Semisweet chocolate chips	1½ cups	375 mL
Vanilla	1 tsp.	5 mL

Put milk, chips and vanilla into saucepan. Melt over medium heat until chips combine when stirred. Remove from heat. Makes 1⅔ cups (400 mL).

DESSERT FONDUE DIPPERS

Strawberries: Remove stems. Cut large berries.

Melon Balls: Make balls or cut into bite size pieces. Use cantaloupe and possibly honeydew and watermelon.

Orange Sections: Tangerines are handy for this purpose. A can of mandarin oranges may be drained and used.

Seedless Grapes: Remove from stems.

Apple Wedges: Dip unpeeled wedges in lemon juice.

Banana Slices: Dip slices in lemon juice unless they are used as soon as cut.

Maraschino Cherries: Drain very well. Blot with paper towels if nec–essary.

Pineapple Chunks: Drain well if using canned.

Cake: Pound cake, angel food cake, doughnuts, rice krispie squares, fruit cake all cut into cubes.

Marshmallows: Use large size. Leave whole or cut in half.

CAESAR SALAD

Another variation of a great salad.

DRESSING

Cooking oil	⅓ cup	75 mL
Garlic clove, quartered	1	1
Egg	1	1
Cider vinegar	2 tbsp.	30 mL
Lemon juice	1 tbsp.	15 mL
Salt	¼ tsp.	1 mL
Pepper	¼ tsp.	1 mL
Anchovy paste	2 tsp.	10 mL
Parmesan cheese	½ cup	125 mL

SALAD

Romaine, medium head	1	1
Lettuce, small head	1	1
Croutons	2 cups	500 mL

Dressing: Combine oil and garlic. Let stand overnight or at least a few hours. Remove garlic. Either discard or chop it finely to add a stronger garlic flavor.

Add remaining ingredients to oil in bowl. Whisk together well. Makes about 1 cup (250 mL).

Salad: Tear greens into bite size pieces into large bowl. Add croutons and dressing. Toss well. Serves 8 or more.

Pare Pointer

We all know how much hippies hate a square dance.

A vibrant orange layer over a creamy base. See the sunrise at mid–night.

Orange flavored gelatin	3 oz.	85 g
Boiling water	1 cup	225 mL
Concentrated frozen orange juice	6 oz.	170 g
Mandarin oranges, well drained (reserve 3 or 4 for garnish)	10 oz.	284 mL
Lemon flavored gelatin	3 oz.	85 g
Boiling water	1 cup	225 mL
Whipping cream (or 1 env. topping)	1 cup	250 mL
Cream cheese, softened	4 oz.	125 g
Mayonnaise for garnish	2 tbsp.	30 mL

In small bowl dissolve orange gelatin in first amount of boiling water. Stir in concentrated orange juice and oranges. Pour into mold. Chill. Stir occasionally to ensure suspension of oranges.

In small bowl, dissolve lemon gelatin in second amount of boiling water. Chill until egg white consistency. Stir 2 or 3 times.

Whip cream until stiff. Blend cream cheese into whipped cream. Fold into thickened lemon gelatin. Pour over top orange layer. Chill well. Unmold on lettuce-lined plate.

Spoon mayonnaise on top center. Add reserved orange sections. Serves 8 to 12.

She's sick. She's a kleptomaniac. Wonder if she takes anything for it.

SHRIMP VELOUTÉ

Prepare early in the day and bake when ready. Freezes well.

Butter or margarine	¼ cup	60 mL
Chopped onion	1 cup	250 mL
Sliced mushrooms	1 cup	250 mL
All-purpose flour	¼ cup	60 mL
Milk	1½ cups	375 mL
Lemon juice	1 tsp.	5 mL
Tomato sauce	3 tbsp.	50 mL
Cooked shrimp	1 lb.	450 g
Sour cream	½ cup	125 mL
Sherry	2 tbsp.	30 mL
Pinch of garlic powder		

Melt butter in frying pan. Add onion and mushrooms. Sauté until onion is soft and clear.

Mix in flour. Add milk, lemon juice and tomato sauce. Heat and stir until it boils and thickens.

Add shrimp, sour cream and sherry. Check for salt and pepper. Add pinch of garlic powder. Turn into 2 quart (2 L) casserole. Bake uncovered in 350°F (180°C) casserole for about 30 minutes until bubbly hot. Serves 4. Double recipe to serve 8.

BAKED RICE

A super easy way to cook rice. Buttery good.

Long grain rice	1½ cups	375 mL
Chicken stock	3 cups	750 mL
Butter or margarine	⅓ cup	75 mL
Parsley flakes	1½ tsp.	7 mL
Salt	¼ tsp.	1 mL
Garlic powder	⅛ tsp.	0.5 mL

Combine all ingredients together in 2 quart (2 L) casserole. Cover and bake in 350°F (180°C) oven for about 40 minutes or until rice is tender. Fluff with fork and serve. Makes 8 servings.

The grand finale for New Year's eve. Make this as simple or as elaborate as you like.

Cake mix, white or chocolate, baked in 2 layers or in 9 × 13 inch (22 × 33 cm) pan	1	1
ICING		
Icing (confectioner's) sugar	3 cups	750 mL
Butter or margarine, softened	6 tbsp.	100 mL
Vanilla	1½ tsp.	7 mL
Water	¼ cup	50 mL
Food coloring		

Beat all together. Add more or less water as needed to make proper spreading consistency.

Tint icing whatever color you like. Ice the cake white and pipe on pink or blue numbers and hands. Ice it with pink icing and pipe on white numbers. Or add ⅓ cup (75 mL) cocoa to some of the icing, then ice cake with chocolate icing and pipe on pink numbers and hands.

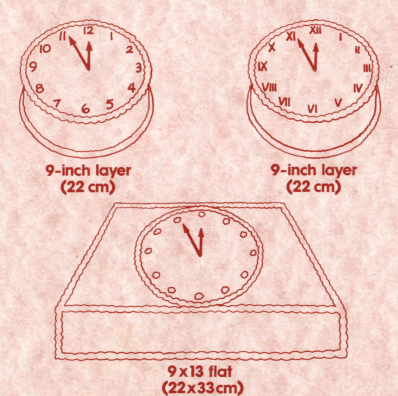

9-inch layer (22 cm)

9-inch layer (22 cm)

9 x 13 flat (22 x 33 cm)

TURKEY VEGETABLE SOUP

Made from the carcass and leftover turkey. Feeds a crowd or fills a freezer.

Turkey carcass, broken up	1	1
Water	14 cups	3 L
Bay leaves	2	2
Salt	1 tbsp.	15 mL
Pepper	¾ tsp.	4 mL
Sugar	1 tsp.	5 mL
Medium carrots, sliced	3	3
Large onion, chopped	1	1
Celery ribs, sliced	6	6
Instant chicken bouillon powder	1 tbsp.	15 mL
Parsley flakes	1 tbsp.	15 mL
Thyme	½ tsp.	2 mL
Long grain rice	½ cup	125 mL
Chopped turkey	2 cups	500 mL

Put turkey carcass, water, bay leaves, salt, pepper and sugar into large pot. Bring to a boil. Cover and simmer for 2 hours. Remove carcass. Discard bay leaves. Return any bits of meat to pot. Discard bones.

Add remaining ingredients. Bring to a boil. Cover and simmer for at least 30 minutes until all vegetables are cooked. Taste for seasoning. Add more water if too thick. Makes about 15 cups (3.4 L).

ICE RING

The secret is sugar-free pop.

Diet soft drink such as Seven Up, ginger ale, orange	4½ cups	1 L

Pour soft drink into mold. A bundt pan makes a very pretty, bubbly looking shape. A salad mold works well also. Be sure to use a soft drink that has no sugar. It will freeze hard and will last longer. If it contains sugar, it will freeze soft and melt quickly. Make several, freeze, unmold and store in plastic bag in freezer.

CANDY CANE COOKIES

If these are wrapped in plastic before hanging on the tree, nibbling is easier to resist.

Butter or margarine, softened	**1 cup**	**250 mL**
Icing (confectioner's) sugar	**1 cup**	**250 mL**
Egg	**1**	**1**
Almond flavoring	**1 tsp.**	**5 mL**
Vanilla flavoring	**1 tsp.**	**5 mL**
Peppermint flavoring	**¼ tsp.**	**1 mL**
All-purpose flour	**2½ cups**	**600 mL**
Baking powder	**1 tsp.**	**5 mL**
Salt	**1 tsp.**	**5 mL**
Red food coloring	**½ tsp.**	**2 mL**

Mix first 6 ingredients together well.

Add flour, baking powder and salt. Mix well.

Divide dough into 2 equal portions. Add food coloring to 1 portion. Blend well. Roll 1 tsp. of each color dough into ropes about 5½ inches (14 cm) long. Lay them side by side. Pinch ends together. Twist to form a spiral. Lay on ungreased baking sheet. Shape top to form a cane. Wreaths are easy to make too. Bake in 350°F (180°C) oven for about 10 minutes until pale gold. Cool on sheet 2 to 3 minutes then remove. Makes about 4½ dozen.

Pictured on page 143.

Paré Pointer

At times we observe someone who seems so patient when in reality it is utter fatigue.

SANTA'S WHISKERS

Rolled in coconut, then chilled, makes this ideal to make one day and bake the next. Good flavor. Chewy.

Butter or margarine, softened	1 cup	250 mL
Granulated sugar	1 cup	250 mL
Vanilla	1 tsp.	5 mL
All-purpose flour	2½ cups	675 mL
Finely chopped candied cherries, red and green	¾ cup	175 mL
Chopped pecans	½ cup	125 mL
Flaked coconut	1 cup	250 mL

Mix first 6 ingredients together well. Shape into 2 rolls 2 inches (5 cm) in diameter.

Roll in coconut. Cover and chill overnight. Next day slice ¼ inch (1 cm) thick. Arrange on ungreased cookie sheet. Bake in 375°F (190°C) oven for about 10 to 12 minutes or until edges are lightly browned. Makes 4 to 5 dozen.

SHORTBREAD

So tender and so mouthwatering and so short lasting.

Butter, softened (not margarine)	1 lb.	454 g
Sugar, half brown, half powdered	¾ cup	175 mL
All-purpose flour	4 cups	900 mL
Colored sugar		
Cherries		

Mix butter, sugar and flour together first with a spoon then work it by hand until it will combine into a ball. Divide into 4 portions. Roll each portion into log about 1¼ inches (3 cm) in diameter. Roll in waxed paper. Chill for shape retention when sliced. May be sliced immedi– ately or rolled on a lightly floured surface and cut into shapes. If slicing, cut in ¼ inch (0.5 cm) rounds. Place on ungreased baking sheet.

Sprinkle with colored sugar or top with a tiny piece of cherry. Bake in 325°F (160°C) oven for 10 to 12 minutes. Makes about 9 dozen.

WHIPPED SHORTBREAD: Using electric mixer, beat butter and sugar well. Slowly beat in flour. Drop by spoonfuls on baking sheet. Press half or whole red or green cherries in center. Bake as above.

FRUIT ROCKS

A most attractive drop cookie with red cherries and nuts showing on top.

Butter or margarine	¹/₂ cup	125 mL
Brown sugar, packed	³/₄ cup	175 mL
Egg	1	1
Vanilla	1 tsp.	5 mL
All-purpose flour	1¹/₄ cups	300 mL
Baking powder	¹/₂ tsp.	2 mL
Salt	¹/₂ tsp.	2 mL
Cinnamon	¹/₂ tsp.	2 mL
Chopped dates	1 cup	250 mL
Candied cherries, cut up	1 cup	250 mL
Candied pineapple ring, cut up	1	1
Chopped walnuts	¹/₂ cup	125 mL
Chopped almonds	¹/₂ cup	125 mL

Cream butter and sugar together well. Beat in egg and vanilla.

Add flour, baking powder, salt and cinnamon. Stir.

Add remaining ingredients. Mix together. Drop by teaspoon onto greased cookie sheet. Bake in 325°F (160°C) oven for about 15 minutes. Makes about 7¹/₂ dozen.

SCOTCH SHORTBREAD

This keeps and keeps. Score your favorite design on top before baking.

Butter, softened	1 lb.	454 g
Granulated sugar	1 cup	225 mL
All-purpose flour	4 cups	900 mL
Vanilla	2 tsp.	10 mL

Combine butter, sugar and about half the flour until mixed. Add rest of flour and vanilla. Work with hands until smooth. Divide into 2 balls. Chill. Press each ball in an 8 inch (20 cm) circle on ungreased baking sheet. Flute edges. Prick with fork here and there. Dough may be flattened to cover jelly roll pan, 10 × 15 inches (25 × 38 cm) instead of 2 separate rounds. Bake in 300°F (150°C) oven for about 45 to 55 minutes or until lightly browned. Let stand for 5 to 10 minutes. Cut into wedges or squares while still warm.

HAYSTACKS

Little stacks of no-bake goodness.

Cream cheese, softened	4 oz.	125 g
Milk	2 tbsp.	30 mL
Icing (confectioner's) sugar	2 cups	500 mL
Unsweetened chocolate square, melted, 1 oz. (28 g) size	1	1
Tiny marshmallows	3 cups	750 mL
Medium coconut		

Beat cheese, milk and icing sugar together until smooth.

Stir in chocolate and marshmallows. Drop by small spoonfuls onto coconut. Roll to cover. Chill on plates. Store in covered container in refrigerator or freezer. Makes about 4 dozen.

Pictured on page 143.

SNOWBALLS

A no-bake cookie. Rolled in coconut to become snowballs

Butter or margarine	2 tbsp.	30 mL
Dates, chopped	1 lb.	454 g
Brown sugar, packed	1 cup	250 mL
Eggs, beaten	2	2
Crisp rice cereal	2 cups	500 mL
Chopped walnuts	1 cup	250 mL
Coconut, long thread		

Put first 4 ingredients into large frying pan. Heat and stir continually until mixture is like fudge. Remove from heat.

Add rice cereal and nuts. With buttered fingers, shape into balls.

Roll balls in coconut. Chill. Makes 4 dozen.

CHERRY CHOCOLATE SQUARES

An exquisite no-bake square. It has a chocolate base and top with a cherry center. So pretty. So special.

BOTTOM LAYER

Butter or margarine	½ cup	125 mL
Granulated sugar	¼ cup	50 mL
Cocoa	⅓ cup	75 mL
Egg, beaten	1	1
Graham cracker crumbs	1¾ cups	400 mL
Coconut	½ cup	125 mL
Walnuts, finely chopped	⅓ cup	75 mL
Water	1 tbsp.	15 mL

SECOND LAYER

Butter or margarine, softened	¼ cup	60 mL
Maraschino cherry juice	2 tbsp.	30 mL
Almond flavoring	1 tsp.	5 mL
Icing (confectioner's) sugar	2 cups	500 mL
Chopped maraschino cherries	⅓ cup	75 mL

THIRD LAYER

Butter or margarine	2 tbsp.	30 mL
Chocolate chips	⅓ cup	75 mL

Bottom Layer: Put butter, sugar and cocoa into heavy saucepan over medium heat. When melted, stir in fork beaten egg and cook until thickened slightly. Remove from heat. Stir in crumbs, coconut, walnuts and water. Press very firmly into ungreased 9 × 9 inch (22 × 22 cm) pan.

Second Layer: Beat butter, cherry juice, almond flavoring and icing sugar together well. Beat slowly at first to keep sugar from flying all over. Blot cherries with paper towels and stir in. Drop dabs here and there over first layer then spread. Let stand for 10 minutes or so. Using your hand, pat smooth.

Third Layer: Melt butter in small saucepan. Add chocolate chips and stir to melt. Pour over top of second layer. With teaspoon, smooth over all. Work quickly so as not to bring any second layer up to the top. Chill. Cuts into 36 squares.

RYLEY'S TOFFEE

Enlist help with the stirring and you will be rewarded with a yummy toffee similar to Ryley's that is no longer available. Wrap each piece in plastic for gifts.

Sweetened condensed milk	11 oz.	300 mL
Brown sugar, packed	1¼ cups	275 mL
Butter	¼ cup	50 mL
Corn syrup	¼ cup	50 mL

Stir all together in heavy saucepan. Bring to boil, stirring continually. Continue to stir and boil over medium-low heat until it reaches the hard ball stage on candy thermometer, 260°F (128°C) or until it forms a hard ball in cold water that chews fairly tough. This sticks to the pan bottom in no time so keep stirring. Pour into well greased 8 × 8 inch (20 × 20 cm) pan. Cool. Cut into squares. This is easier to do if toffee is scored with knife before too hard. When cold remove from pan. Break over edge of counter or sink.

Pictured on page 143.

GRAND MARNIER BALLS

A good size chocolate treat. Brandy or rum flavoring with water may easily be substituted for the Grand Marnier.

Whipping cream	¾ cup	175 mL
Butter or margarine	¼ cup	50 mL
Granulated sugar	3 tbsp.	50 mL
Grand Marnier (or condensed orange juice)	3 tbsp.	50 mL
Semisweet chocolate squares, melted 1 oz. (28 g) size	7	7
Chocolate graham cracker crumbs or other chocolate cookie crumbs	3 cups	700 mL
Chocolate sprinkles		

(continued on next page)

Put cream, butter and sugar into saucepan over medium heat. Bring to boil, stirring often. Remove from heat.

Add Grand Marnier, chocolate and crumbs. Mix well. Chill.

Shape into 42 balls. Roll in chocolate sprinkles. Chill or freeze. Makes 3½ dozen.

RUM BALLS: Use rum or rum flavoring plus water instead of Grand Marnier.

Pictured on page 143.

RUM ROLLS

Melt-in-your-mouth treats that don't stay on a tray very long. May also be shaped into balls.

Butter or margarine, softened	½ cup	125 mL
Icing (confectioner's) sugar	1½ cups	375 mL
Semisweet chocolate chips	¾ cup	175 mL
Eggs	2	2
Rum flavoring	1 tsp.	5 mL
Water	2 tbsp.	30 mL
Chocolate wafer cookies, crushed into crumbs	1¾ cups	425 mL
Colored fancies (tiny colored bead decoration)		
Chocolate sprinkles		

Combine butter, icing sugar and chocolate chips in saucepan. Heat and stir to melt.

Add eggs. Stir until thickened. Remove from heat.

Stir in rum flavoring, water and crumbs. Scrape into foil lined bowl and chill. It will seem very granular at this point.

Divide dough into 3 parts. It will be almost hard as a rock. Squeeze, knead and work dough until it can be shaped. Roll into a log about 1½ inches (4 cm) in diameter. Roll in colored or chocolate sprinkles. Store in plastic bag in refrigerator. Slice to use.

Pictured on page 143.

PECAN BALLS

A bite of one of these little round balls will lead to more. They melt in your mouth.

Butter or margarine, softened	1 cup	250 mL
Icing (confectioner's) sugar	½ cup	125 mL
All-purpose flour	2¼ cups	550 mL
Ground pecans	1 cup	250 mL
Vanilla	2 tsp.	10 mL
Icing (confectioner's) sugar	½ cup	125 mL

Combine first 5 ingredients in bowl. Mix first with spoon then by hand to work it until it holds together. Shape into small balls. Arrange on ungreased baking sheet. Bake in 325°F (160°C) oven for 20 to 25 minutes.

As soon as balls have cooled enough to handle, roll them in icing sugar. Makes about 6 dozen.

ALMOND BALLS: Omit pecans. Add 1 cup (250 mL) ground almonds.

ALMOND CRESCENTS: Omit pecans. Add 2 cups (500 mL) ground almonds. Roll into ropes as thick as your finger. Cut into 2 inch (5 cm) lengths. Pinch ends to taper. Shape into crescents.

BURIED CHERRY: Completely cover well drained maraschino cherries with dough. Bake same as above.

CHRISTMAS